Wired to Work

Answering the Two Most Important Questions in Life

by

Vince D'Acchioli

Huntington House Publishers

Huntington House Publishers
P.O. Box 53788
Lafayette, Louisiana 70505

PRINTED IN THE UNITED STATES OF AMERICA.

Library of Congress Control Number 2001092107
ISBN 1-56384-191-6

Contents

Foreword

We humans face an inescapable irony. We're so adept at achieving mastery in life's "externals" (e.g., outer space, cyber-space, atomic physics or quantum mechanics, etc.), yet we still struggle so much with life's "internals."

I mean, from everything domestic (marriage, kids, money) to our business pursuits, struggles still crowd in, choke out or break things down. Across the full spectrum of "internal" issues, from *self-control* (managing such things as temper, eating habits, moral integrity), to *prioritizing* (like scheduling life without mechanizing it to a point of self-destruct), our skills tend to sag—sometimes disastrously.

You may have it all down tight, but not so with the majority. In fact, as a speaker to tens of thousands at a time, and a one-at-a-time counselor to thousands over the years, I'm convinced: none of us are without need of help getting in touch with and managing "the internals." I don't think we can be, at once, upright honest and downright smug about ourselves and not admit our human vulnerability to "missing it," or "botching it up," or "blowing it out our ear." Sooner than later, I think we all ask ourselves, "Isn't life supposed to work different from this?"

In this context, I refer to "life" as something more than simply making a buck, a sale or a reputation for smarts, savvy or social success. I mean to address what this book does: "The way things were supposed to be," or at least, "what I (we or most people) always hoped, dreamed or thought I could plan it to be." But when it doesn't, we either try to re-invent our lives (which no one really can, not on durable terms), or opt for some human program of achievement, recovery or improvement (which is destined to come up short and return us to the original question).

When I first met Vince D'Acchioli, some twenty years ago, this is where he was. As he walked into the place I was serving, he was a guy hitting on all eight cylinders business wise—"knockin' 'em dead" in the corporate world. But personal issues were crowding him to come to honest terms with the fact that *externals* never substitute for the *internals*. And that honesty crowded him to come to terms with the *eternals*. Vince met Jesus Christ. Having become realistic with his limits at success in marriage, his family, and other issues of integrity with his personal life, he then began to discover how his relationship with God did more than bring inspiration—he found the Life-giver brought him in touch with practical concepts for living life.

As Vince began to get a handle on these *keys*—keys that make life work—I had the joy of watching him from the sidelines as a pastor-coach. Having learned that real "success" in life looks different from what he always thought, he gradually began to help others. With time, he has become uniquely gifted at sharing those "keys" with others and helping them learn how to use them. When that happened, people began finding their lives getting "on target," which has now become the name of Vince's organization. I like what he's doing now, and there's a reason.

Though I'm a pastor and spiritual leader, I've always had a disaffection for anything that suggests God is either a stained-glass mystery or that He is hunting for the "religiously inclined." So you can imagine my pleasure with this book, where Vince as the author, offers nothing of the suffocating "religious," or smugly "know-it-all." But you will find a solid, fulfilling infusion of "the right stuff"—practical, non-preachy and workable.

Wired to Work is a toolbox that summarizes the practical principles always intended for our understanding—the *principles that can enable you or me to actually become what we were created to be*. If you are among the insightful, who more and more are discovering we can't skirt, avoid or toss these concepts aside, you're going to like this book. You have in hand a development of those principles—presented and applied in ways that justify the title: *they'll "work."*

So open the toolbox . . . and get started. You won't find a more useful resource to build your relationships—from life's fundamental "connect point" with God, to making all other relationships work, and finding goals begin to become more realizable than you ever dreamed. It's called, "experiencing life the way it was always intended—the way it was "wired to work."

Jack W. Hayford
Pastor / Chancellor
The Church On The Way
The King's College and Seminary

PS: Incidentally, if anyone wonders how "real" Vince is, let me add—the man is genuine from the ground up, and he and his wife Cindy have bundles of good and great stuff to offer wherever they go today. They're what I call "functional disciples" of the ultimate Master, Jesus Christ. His "amazing grace" explains the quality of their lives; commitment and passionate commitment to servant-heartedness and Vince's growth as a leader helping others make life work.

Acknowledgments

I want to start by acknowledging the most special person in my life, my lovely wife, Cindy. Your unconditional love, your dedication through times of trial, and your incredible patience over thirty-five years of marriage stand as a model for what it means to be a Godly woman. I love you with all of my heart!

In addition, I would like to thank my two beautiful daughters, Kimberly and Kristen. My heart is overflowing with emotion as I think about your commitment to me and to our ministry over these past several years. Thank you for always believing in me and for investing a part of your life towards the fulfillment of God's plan and purpose for our family. You are so loved!

In regards to this book, I want to specifically thank Kristen, my current office manager and full-time editor. With your literary expertise and strong attention to detail, you managed to turn this speaker into a writer. Without your many hours of hard work this project would not have been possible.

I also want to thank my pastor and dear friend, Dr. Jack Hayford. Your exemplary life, and the teaching which flows from it, have contributed more to my personal growth as a man than any other single influence in my life. I am so appreciative of your continual mentorship and support.

Finally, I would like to acknowledge several incredibly gifted friends and family members who have contributed their valuable time and ideas to help make this book a reality. They are listed as follows:

Allen Rowe
Bob and Sue Grant
Brad and Ann Fallentine
Dean and Lori Jones
Jack and Mary Duitsman
Jerry and Dixie Melchisedeck
Mark McWilliams
Rich and Linda Simons
Rick and Robin Brink
Ron and Leslie D'Acchioli
Ted and Debi Heiden
Timothy Bailey

Thank you dear ones. Your labor of love is much appreciated!

Introduction

Thirty-five years of combined experience in business and ministry has led me to the discovery of some important truths. I believe with all my heart that what you are about to read contains the keys to living a secure, happy, and fulfilled life. Whether it is your personal life, your marriage, or your career, the principles that you will discover in this book *will* have a profound and lasting impact.

The Struggle

Ever since the fall of man, we have all been engaged in a lifelong search for security. From the time that Adam and Eve first covered themselves with fig leaves, humankind has been on a quest for safety and protection. Each one of us has an innate desire to feel safe and secure. Security is primarily significant as it often allows us the freedom to seek our second basic need, the need for purpose and meaning in life. Unfortunately, today many are looking in all the wrong places. Drugs, alcohol, sexual addiction, and a preoccupation with materialism (all providing a temporary sense of satisfaction) are just a few of the contemporary traps we fall into in our quest for answers.

The Hope

Over the past thirty years I have involved myself in the observance and study of human behavior. In doing so, one question invariably came to mind, "Why are some people happy, secure, successful, and making a difference in their world while others seem to struggle?" I made it my goal to pursue the answer to this question, setting out to reveal the transferable characteristics these successful people seemed to possess. As I began to focus on these role models, I found that most had three things in common.

First, they had an intimate relationship with God. (In this book whenever I refer to God, I do not mean "a god," but rather God, "The Father," the Judeo Christian God.) I want to emphasize that word *intimate.* Most of us, especially men, have a difficult time understanding intimacy. Second, they had successfully answered *the two most important questions in life*, they knew exactly *how* and *why* God made them; they had *vision.* Third, they were living out the vision. They were *doing* what they were designed to do.

My main purpose in writing this book is to encourage you to strive toward the achievement of these three objectives; to give you the principles that you must understand in order to be all that God has made you to be, and to ultimately help you answer the two most important questions in life:

1) Lord, *how* did You make me uniquely? (How am I *wired*? What are my *natural* areas of giftedness? When You look at me, what do You see?)

2) *Why* am I here? (What is Your purpose, *vision*, for my life? What is my life's *work*?)

As I deliver this message throughout the US and Canada, I continue to witness the tremendous change that takes place in people's hearts and lives once they have unraveled the answers to these two questions. The result is nothing short of incredible!

I don't know about you, but quite often I find myself wishing that God would just descend from heaven, grab me by my lapels and say, "Listen Vince, this is how

I made you . . . this is how I see you . . . and here is what I want you to do."

Throughout history *vision* has proven to be the driving force behind most success. If you study most of the people we look up to as heroes, great leaders, and role models, you will discover that at the core of their life was a deep and sustained sense of purpose and vision.

God's Plan

God's greatest desire for you and me is to see ourselves as He sees us and then to discover the vision that He has for our lives. Once we catch that vision, I believe He steps back, gets a big smile on His face, and looks on in great anticipation as the vision begins to impact our lives and everything we do. You see, I don't think that God is primarily interested in our future goals and objectives. His number one desire for us is to catch the vision, His vision for our lives!

Three Unalterable Facts

At On Target Ministries, we have adopted what I call the "Three Unalterable Facts." These facts form the core around which our ministry and this book are founded. These three facts are as follows:

First, God knows you and has created you for a special purpose. God made you. You are not some random experiment. You are created in His image and for His purpose.

Second, God has given you special gifts toward the satisfaction of His purpose. You are unique, designed with an amazing, one-of-a-kind set of spiritual DNA. By functioning within your God-given gifts, you can realize the reason you were created.

Third, God wants you to discover what His purpose is, His vision for your life.

Later in this book we will break these facts down

further and look at the overwhelming biblical support behind each one.

Before We Begin

If you have come this far, you are probably one of the millions of men and women in search of real purpose and meaning in life. Perhaps you are a Christian and have been in a meaningful relationship with God for a long time, but now you want to get a new sense of His purpose for your life. Maybe you are a new believer struggling to discover how to make sense of the dichotomy between a vision that is shaped by the world around you, your current circumstances, and God's plan for your life. Or maybe you are on the fence, and not sure if God is even real.

No matter where you are coming from, I believe that there is something significant for you in the pages that follow. Before we begin this journey together, I would like to make one request, one that you may find a little unusual. I want to ask you to pray and ask God to reveal something special to you as you read this book. If you are like me, you know that books are like events—they do not usually bring about meaningful and lasting change. They do, however, contain useful information that is often buried like hidden treasure. I suggest that you ask God to reveal those one or two precious nuggets He intends for you to glean from your time spent in this book.

Also, I have included at the end of each chapter a summry of that chapter and a section for discussion and comment. I hope you find this helpful.

Lord, don't let me miss what You want to say to me through these pages . . .

Or for you it may be, *Lord, if You're real, please help me to come to a better understanding of just who You are . . .*

Chapter One

One Man's Struggle—Every Person's Hope

In 1965, I began working my way up the ranks of a major retail operation based in southern California. I did well, and by the age of thirty-nine I had become a corporate vice-president. Along with the fancy title came all of the usual trappings of success, a new car and boat in the garage, a newly remodeled house, and fabulous vacations. My family life was impressive as well. I was blessed with a wonderful wife who never ceased to amaze me with her unconditional loyalty and love, and together we shared two incredible daughters, Kimberly and Kristen.

From the outside looking in, my life seemed flawless. But beneath it all, there was a void in my heart—something was missing. I had no clue what it was. In fact, I never even took the time to think about it. I was much too busy planning out my next promotion and thinking about what my next new toy might be. Looking back, I could sense that something was missing, but it took me years to figure out just what that was. As I share my story, perhaps you'll discover why.

The Early Days

I was born in 1945 in Cranston, Rhode Island, the eldest of three children. My brother Ron came along two years later, and my sister Patti completed the pack after another five years. While our nuclear family was small, we had a large extended family living on the East Coast, mostly relatives on my father's side.

If you guessed "D'Acchioli" is Italian, you guessed right. Heritage was extremely important among my relatives. You have to understand that back in the 40s and 50s when you were born into an east coast Italian family, there were some rules. First, you must be outspokenly proud of your heritage. Second, you must remain Catholic from cradle to grave. And last but not least, in matters of politics, you must function as a loyal Democrat. Oh yes, and it was always to your benefit to know how to play the accordion by the ripe old age of four. Those were the rules.

Because I was the first born of my father's generation, everyone in the extended family lavished me with attention. This was especially true of my grandmother who lived with us and was often called on to care for me while mom and dad were at work. Without intending to, she really spoiled me. I was given just about anything I asked for. As you might imagine, this made life difficult for mom and dad. I was used to getting my own way, and if I didn't, a temper tantrum was soon to follow. The sad part was that more often than not, my little fits would cause mom and dad to give in. As a result, I learned early on how to be a controlling person and how to manipulate situations through my behavior.

In 1953, my parents announced that we were going to take a two-week trip to California to visit some of mom's relatives. Money was tight, so this vacation seemed beyond our wildest dreams. We excitedly piled into the old Nash Rambler (the car that looked like a big bullet) and headed across the country bound for the West Coast.

Little did I know that was the last time I would ever see my childhood home. We never made it back to Rhode Island. My parents, who had been experiencing deep financial difficulties, decided to make a fresh start in the Los Angeles area.

For the first several years, we lived with relatives who had ventured out to California ahead of us. I must have been pretty irresistible, because it did not take long to add the new family members to the list of folks I already had wrapped around my little finger.

At the appropriate age, my parents enrolled me in the Catholic school system, a nightmare for a boy who had turned misbehavior into an art form! Catholic schools in those days were strict, especially for an undisciplined kid like me. My colorful personality caught the attention of more than one nun, and the painful end of more than one yardstick.

Upon turning thirteen, I started working part-time for my dad in a local paint store. Sweeping floors and stocking shelves for a little spending money was a small taste of freedom. But on the school front, I was still considered a discipline problem, so much so that I was asked to leave my Catholic high school before the year was over. Not only was I a challenge to control, I was flunking out with four *F*s and a *D*. (I liked to brag that the D was in religion.)

With no nuns in sight, disciplinary action in my new public school was lax, and I took advantage of this by goofing off whenever and wherever the opportunity arose. I smoked, raced my new hot rod around campus, and prided myself on being an all-around nuisance. The call to the principal's office became quite a familiar tune.

I remember one specific incident where my buddies and I cut school to go to Mount Wilson to watch the snowfall, an unusual event for southern California. While taking in the view, we failed to notice a local news crew capturing the event on film. That night, I settled into the living room with my dad to watch a little television. You guessed it. Right in the middle of the evening news the camera flashed on the back of my car, license plate and all. Ouch!

Falling in Love

In spite of all of the trouble, there was one good thing that came out of those high school years. That is when I met a beautiful young girl named Cindy Heiden. She came from a very loving family, and, in character, she was everything that I was not . . . soft-spoken, sensitive, and extremely sweet. I managed to catch her attention with my class-clown antics and adventuresome spirit. Before long I was courting my own blonde, blue-eyed "Sandra Dee."

However, after dating Cindy for just a short time, my personality began to suffocate her in many ways. A total lack of discipline in my life had produced a stubborn, macho, have-to-have-it-my-way Italian guy with an overly dominant personality. Since neither of us had a personal relationship with God, our lives began to head in different directions, and there was no road map in sight.

In spite of the circumstances, we somehow managed to keep things together. Graduation could not come fast enough for two love struck teenagers. In 1965, fresh out of high school, Cindy and I were married.

In tying the knot so quickly, we had unknowingly set the stage for disaster. Cindy was the first person in the history of my family to test the rules. She was

German, came from a Lutheran background and was very conservative politically. Interestingly enough, she did play the accordion. That must be a German thing, too.

It was at this point that my life began to take a serious turn for the worse. The accumulation of years of looking up to all the wrong role models took its toll. I was living a secret life full of drinking, adultery, and cheating any way that I could. I was also dangerously close to becoming involved in organized crime.

With the new responsibility of married life, I began to work forty hours at the paint store and enrolled in college on a part-time basis. During this time, I recall one particular weekend when Cindy and I decided to drop by her mom's house for a visit. Cindy's younger brother Ted greeted us and excitedly shared the news that he had just accepted Jesus at a Campus Crusade for Christ meeting. He couldn't stop talking about his born-again experience.

Ted's conversion deeply affected Cindy. Unbeknownst to me, she had been quietly seeking the Lord for some time. When she saw the joy on her brother's face (a fellow who had not long before been caught growing marijuana in the family birdbath) she knew the change was real. Shortly thereafter, Cindy made her own personal commitment to the Lord. At the time, I remember thinking that my wife had become some sort of Jesus freak. Her attempts to share the good news with me were often met with an enthusiastic, "Leave me out of it!"

From that point on, our lives continued to head in opposite directions, only this time it was happening at a more accelerated pace. One friend actually told Cindy, "I can't ever see Vince coming to know Jesus—never!" Another friend counseled her to give up and abandon the marriage.

As hopelessness set in, I gradually began to notice a change in Cindy's life. Out of sheer curiosity I agreed to accompany her to a Wednesday night Bible study at an old fraternity house located near the UCLA campus. The leader was a man named Hal Lindsey.

"Who's he?" I asked.

"He's just written a book called *The Late Great Planet Earth*," replied Cindy. "I think you'll like him."

When we arrived at the meeting, the old frat house was already packed with young people. We struggled to find a place on the floor to sit. I could feel the energy and excitement in the air. Before long, a tall, rugged-looking guy, wearing a black leather jacket, opened the meeting with his testimony. What a colorful character he was. He had been a successful stuntman and revealed a former connection to the Mafia. He had also put in time in Vietnam as an assassin. He explained how he turned to drugs after being injured and ended up living with witches. Then he went on to share how accepting Christ had changed his life. His persona completely blew my stereotype of what a Christian was. I was not about to call *this* guy a Jesus freak.

I was even more impressed with the teaching of Hal Lindsey. He made the Bible come alive! Seeds were being sown, but I wasn't ready to let them take root, at least not yet.

The Decision

A few months later, on my commute home from work, I took some time to reflect on my life. I had just been promoted to store manager in Pasadena. My company stock was booming and I was right in line for the next promotion. My outlook was as bright as the sunny Southern California climate. But something gnawed at my conscience. Suddenly, I had an overwhelming sense that if I did not get serious about God right at that moment, I might never have a second chance.

As I sat in bumper-to-bumper traffic that afternoon, I knew I had to make a decision. I began to pray, "Lord, if You're real, I want You in my life. I want what these other people have." When I got home, I proudly announced this event to Cindy. She was thrilled! She recalled the wonderful effect that this conversion had on her brother's life and could not wait to see the evidence of change in mine.

Sadly, Cindy's optimism was soon crushed. Although I professed to be a believer, *my life did not change.* I did not read the Bible, pray, or even attend church on a regular basis. You see, I accepted Jesus as my Savior—but not as my Lord. For eight long years I rode the fence with one foot in the world and one foot in the kingdom.

At work, I continued to be promoted to the level of district manager. Along with this title came the management responsibility for a dozen or so stores and hundreds of employees. They were all accountable to me. The new position also required a significant amount of travel. And as is often the case, the time spent apart from my family soon gave way to temptation. When I was not tied up in meetings, I was drawn to the local bars and pool halls. My secret life continued.

I was living the life of a hypocrite, professing to be a Christian while immersing myself in sinful behavior. I tell people now that I did more damage for the kingdom as a new believer than I did before I knew God. In accepting Christ, my life did not change and that was quite obvious to the two to three thousand employees who now worked for me on a daily basis. They knew of my newfound faith, but I was not producing the fruit that they expected to see.

Which God Do I Want?

To quote my friend Pat Morely, "There is a God we *want* . . . and there is the God who *is*, and they are not the same God." You see, like many, I was pursuing the God I *wanted*, the one who does not care about compromises. I learned to justify my shortcomings and became quite an expert at interpreting the Bible in such a way that it affirmed my lifestyle. This is where I was.

Breaking Point

Then came the breaking point. Cindy uncovered the secrets in my life that I was struggling to keep hidden. For the first time, there was no way to manipulate myself out of this predicament. A pastor friend of mine used to always say, "There is no such thing as a secret." What an incredible truth! God's giant searchlight had landed on my sinful path, and I was dangerously close to losing the people I loved most in life, my wife and my children.

By the time I finally hit bottom, I had already inflicted an incredible amount of pain on Cindy. I remember pleading with her, stating that I would do whatever it took to salvage our relationship and turn my life around. This time I meant it! It took absolute desperation to get my attention. I had to be crushed.

Seeing a New Start

Over the next week or so, Cindy and I didn't communicate much. She spent hours weeping and crying out to the Lord for guidance. He became her source of comfort, and in her spirit she felt Him telling her, "Be still and quiet. I am wrestling with Vince's soul."

In the midst of this time of trial, Cindy and our two girls had been attending the Church On The Way located in Van Nuys, California. I knew very little about this church other than Cindy's fondness for Pastor Jack

Hayford. In pursuit of spiritual and marital healing, I agreed to attend several counseling sessions with one of the associate pastors.

I'll never forget that first appointment. We poured out our hearts and then waited for our counselor's response. He paused and then turned to Cindy,

"What are you going to do?" he asked.

"I don't know," replied Cindy.

"What did Jesus do for you?" asked the associate pastor.

Cindy's response was immediate, "He went to the cross."

"Then what?"

Cindy paused for a moment and responded, "He died."

The counselor's next words would reverberate in my mind for years to come. He turned to me and said, "Vince, I want you to look into your wife's eyes." I did as he suggested and stared into her eyes for an uncomfortable amount of time (for us guys that's anything more than four seconds). The counselor continued, "It has been said that you can tell the character of a man by looking into the eyes of his wife. I don't see much life in there, do you?"

I was cut to the core. In that moment God gave me a panoramic view of the immense hurt and pain that I had heaped upon this precious child of His. I cannot remember a time when I ever felt so ashamed. I repented for my sins, and was extremely grateful when my wife agreed to stay and work things out.

Cindy now shares how God whispered to her heart in a clear but inaudible voice, "If you will forgive Vince—I promise you there will be a third-day resurrection." Right then, she made a decision that would have a lasting impact on our future together—she decided to forgive me and place the past behind us.

Realizing that forgiveness is never a one time event, I knew that it would take a lot of time to process the pain and hurt. Week by week, step by step, spiritual growth took place. I remained committed to do whatever it took to change—to truly repent—to turn 180 degrees from my past. I desperately wanted to salvage my family. That meant everything to me.

The Bible tells us in Acts 2:38, to repent and be baptized. There is a powerful purpose in coupling these two acts of obedience. We may *decide* to repent, but the Lord knows that we need His supernatural power to pull it off. For me, that power came when I chose to be baptized. This life-altering decision came in response to one of Pastor Hayford's clear and compelling sermons regarding the need for obedience in this area.

Having been brought up in the Roman Catholic tradition where baptism meant sprinkling an infant with a few drops of water, the idea of being fully immersed was quite foreign to me. Regardless, I was obedient. And when that day came, God performed something magnificent in my heart.

He reached down and washed me clean. He stripped away all my guilt and condemnation. For the very first time, I was finally able to let go of my past. I felt like a new man! The old lifestyle and patterns were no longer relevant, and I set out to live my life as a new creation in Christ. I was truly overwhelmed by the grace of God.

The Search for Meaning and Purpose

Cindy patiently looked on as my level of integrity began to grow. When lowbrow TV shows would come on, she waited to see if I was going to change the channel, and with a newfound sense of conviction I did. I also started to make a habit of studying the Bible and incorporating God's Word into my life. In fact, He became my spiritual CEO.

Not only was I growing spiritually, but on the job my leadership skills were flourishing as well. After thirteen years at the paint company, I was named (the youngest ever) corporate vice-president. What an honor!

Unfortunately, just a few years following my promotion, the company shifted business philosophies and began to slowly deteriorate. We had to borrow two hundred million dollars to protect ourselves from a hostile takeover. As an officer of the company, I remember sitting in a conference room high atop an L.A. skyscraper with scores of lawyers, bankers, accountants and company executives to sign for that loan. The interest payments alone were staggering.

The company changed after that, and I began to feel that my time of service was drawing to a close. I remember praying, "Lord, there must be something else for me. I need to know exactly where You want me, and please do not offer me too many choices, or I am likely to take the wrong path."

It was at this crossroads that I began to process the importance of understanding *how* and *why* God made me. I sought to understand the differences between vocational and personal satisfaction. In doing so, I uncovered the contrast between our learned vs. our natural gifts and how sometimes our learned behavior can suffocate God's natural gifting in us. I also learned some important principles to discovering *real* purpose in life. Later you will read about two vocational transitions that helped me understand the secrets to a happy and fulfilled life.

A Final Word

Before you begin the next chapter, I find it imperative to make a couple of suggestions. I am going to begin by discussing the necessity of a close personal relationship with God as critical to our ultimate understanding of His purpose for our lives. There are two main obstacles that stand in the way of most people experiencing this kind of intimacy with Him. First, is our inability to effectively process and let go of our past. I am talking about the crippling effect of past negative life experiences. This area could be the subject of an entire book, therefore I cannot do it justice with a few casual comments. I will say this, if you are struggling with issues like fear, anger, unforgiveness, and guilt, you need to pursue release from your past. There are many fine resources in your local bookstore.

The second issue is obedience. It is one thing to let go of your past and another to learn to live a disciplined, obedient life so as not to accumulate more negative experiences. Obedience is a major issue. God both desires and has given us ways to bring about obedience in our life. The first way is to take charge, get tough and practice saying no to temptations. It is possible to do this in your own strength—but extremely difficult. This is where most people struggle. You have made countless attempts to overcome that obstacle—maybe even come close at times—but you seem to end up right back where you were. We need to take our cue from the Apostle Paul who in 1 Corinthians 9:24-27 talks about how he must beat his body and make it his slave.

Let me conclude by sharing one thing that worked for me. You may remember that I was baptized about a week after Cindy and I met with the counselor. What happened to me after the baptism is hard to explain. Each of us has been given the power to make choices. However, in the real world we face temptations that are so influential that they can overwhelm us and cause us to make the wrong choices. In my case, after that baptism, there was a power available to me that I had never experienced. I realized that the Holy Spirit now residing in me would be my most significant help in overcoming temptations.

You see, I believe that you can go only so far on your own. But when you accept Jesus in your heart and are baptized, you have acquired another resource to overcome temptations. As I said, I do not pretend to know how this works, but I can tell you I have experienced it first hand. My encouragement to you is that if you have not accepted the Lord into your life and been obedient in baptism—do it now! It is critical to your ability to overcome life's obstacles and ultimately discover *how* and *why* God made you.

Chapter Summary:

1. The things we learn from our early years of growing up can become powerful forces that shape how we live our lives.
2. Some people have to experience a major life-altering event in order for God to get their attention.
3. God can redeem any situation—His grace is sufficient and His mercies are new every morning. He is the God of new beginnings.
4. Through conversion and baptism, God gives us the additional power to overcome temptations.

Discussion Questions:

1. Where am I right now in my relationship with my family and with God?
2. What are the one or two things I learned from this chapter that can help me avoid making similar mistakes in my own life?

Write down one or two key ideas that you gleaned from this chapter and at least one new behavior you would like to start practicing.

Key Ideas

____

____

____

____

New Behavior/Commitment

____

____

____

____

Coming Up in Chapter Two:

The next chapter will discuss the key to everything—getting to know God and understanding why a close relationship with Him is essential if we are to ever discover the answers to the two most important questions in life.

Chapter Two

Getting to Know Your Very Best Friend

Patrick Means tells an amazing story in his book, *Men's Secret Wars*: "A nun was working in a men's prison. One spring an inmate asked the nun to buy him a Mother's Day card to send home. She agreed. But word traveled fast in the prison; soon hundreds of inmates were asking for cards. So the nun contacted a greeting card manufacturer, who happily sent crates of Mother's Day cards to the prison. All the cards were passed out.

Soon afterward the nun realized that Father's Day was approaching and, thinking ahead, once again called the card manufacturer, who responded quickly with crates of Father's Day cards. Years later, the nun explained that she still had every one of them. Not one prisoner requested a card for his father."

What an incredible testimony of the absence of a father figure. It has been said that we are experiencing a "father vacuum" in this country. The lack of a healthy father figure to help young people in their growth and development is having a profound impact upon our culture.

My Real Dad

My father and I did not have the kind of intimate relationship I would have liked. I recall the deep sadness I felt when he died in 1983 and sometimes still feel when I think of him. I have come to realize that God's plan has always been for our earthly fathers to model Him. Often the greatest hindrance to people seeing their *real* Heavenly Father is dysfunctional relationships with their earthly fathers.

In my case, the hole in my heart brought about by a less than perfect relationship with my dad, was never filled until I discovered my *real* daddy—my Heavenly Father. This discovery has so impacted my life that I now believe an intimate relationship with God is the ultimate fulfillment in life—the secret to everything. Perhaps this idea is a stretch for you. I want to encourage you to read on with an open mind and heart. What I am about to unfold in this chapter could revolutionize your life. If you choose to live out what I am suggesting here—I promise you—you will soon discover *how* and *why* God made you.

Your Best Friend

Building an intimate relationship with God is a topic that I speak about quite regularly. I title this message, "*Getting to know your best friend.*" How would you describe your best friend? I find that when I am very close to someone, I often begin to behave and talk a little bit like him or her. Have you ever found yourself doing that? At times you may even take on a few of their mannerisms. I believe this happens when we come across a person whom we can easily love, admire, and respect.

This is why we need to get close to Jesus. God's greatest desire is for Jesus to be seen in us. If we want to make Jesus our best friend, we must begin to see Him in the same way we view those special people around us. We must spend time with Him.

Let's suppose that you had a life and death issue that you were dealing with right now and that you really needed someone to be there for you. The likelihood of you choosing to contact someone outside of your inner circle of family or friends would be very small. You would never feel free to share your heart with someone you did not know. How could you trust them? How would they respond? As Christians, if we do not know God intimately, we are not likely to turn to Him for guidance and direction. We cannot trust and rely upon a Lord that we have not taken the time to get to know. Do you want a best friend who will never fail you, who knows you better than anyone else, and who is able to provide you with a lasting sense of fulfillment and purpose? Get close to God!

"You will never rely upon someone you do not trust— and you will never trust someone you do not know."

In Matthew 14: 28-30 Peter called out, "Lord, if it is You tell me to come to You on the water." The Lord answered Peter and he confidently stepped out of the boat and walked on the water. Peter considered Jesus his closest friend, so much so that he was willing to trust Him with his life. He literally walked on the water! What a phenomenal evidence of unconditional love and trust. But we all know that the story did not stop there. As long as Peter had his eyes fixed on Jesus, his feet stayed above the water. However, the minute he looked away and let fear and doubt enter his mind, he began to sink.

Each day we face the same decision that Peter faced as he walked across that water. We can choose to keep our eyes on Jesus or focus on the circumstances around us. We must discover how to never doubt God's ability to handle even the smallest of cares in our life. We live in a world where the temptation to take control of our own situation is always going to exist. Even so, God promises us something much greater than our best effort could ever produce. First Peter 5:6 instructs, "Humble yourselves, therefore, under the mighty hand of God, that He may exalt you at the proper time, casting all your anxiety upon Him, because He cares for you." Philippians 4:6-7 reminds us once again, "Be anxious for nothing, but in everything by prayer and supplication with thanksgiving let your requests be made known to God. And the peace of God, which surpasses all comprehension, shall guard your hearts and minds in Christ Jesus."

My wife led me to a significant realization. She taught me that it is okay to go to God for *everything*. Let me explain. One day as Cindy and I were pulling into the parking lot of our local McDonalds, she suggested that we pray for a parking spot. My immediate response was, "What, pray for a parking spot? Give me a break! God doesn't care about parking spots." Just then, somebody backed out of the premier spot of the lot (that prized space right next to the first handicap spot). My wife said nothing. She just sat there with that "I told you so" smile on her face. As I have watched her do this over and over, I have learned that no concern is too small in the eyes of God. We can turn to Him with anything.

Like a Hand in a Glove

Psalm 16:8 says, " I have set the Lord always before me." What does this mean? To set the Lord always before you means to allow Him to be the driving force in your life. In my seminars I often bring this point home with the use of a baseball mitt. There are several different types of mitts available. Serious baseball players would probably choose their gloves according to the position they were going to play. An outfielder or pitcher's glove would be needed to snag those long fly balls. A first basemen's glove would need to be able to scoop the ball out of the dirt when it comes to first base. A catcher's mitt must be equipped with a little extra padding in order to take the heat.

As is the case with each individual glove, you and I have also been designed for a unique purpose. It is important to understand that a baseball glove is nothing more than a useless piece of leather without a hand to guide it. A person's hand enables that glove to work for a particular purpose—its intended purpose. In much the same way, we are nothing more than a physical body unless the Lord is working in and through us. As our Creator, He is the only one who understands how we work, and therefore He is the only one who is able to direct us toward the fulfillment of our intended purpose.

Perhaps this has happened to you. You are playing catch—warming up before the game. You take off your glove to adjust your cap or uniform and someone throws the ball at you, unaware that you do not have your glove on. There is no time to prepare. So what do you do? You take the glove and throw it at the ball—hoping to knock it down so you won't have to chase it. Some of us are trying to navigate through life in much the same way. If God's hand is not in our glove (life), we will spend the rest of our lives chasing obstacles.

What's the Answer?

So how do we go about insuring that God's hand is always in our glove? How do we start the process?

Well, the first thing we need to do is to realize the importance of *letting go*. Paul talks about this in 2 Corinthians 12:8-9. Referring to a thorn or struggle in his life he states, "Three times I've pleaded with the Lord to take it away." God's answer to Paul was simply, "My grace is sufficient for you, for my power is made perfect in weakness." His response was immediate, Paul continues, "Therefore I'll boast all the more gladly about my weaknesses, for when I am weak, then I am strong." Like Paul, we need to understand our absolute poverty to make things happen on our own. We must allow God to orchestrate our circumstances. Matthew 10:39 reminds us, "Whoever finds his life will lose it, whoever loses his life for my sake will find it."

I came across this tender poem not too long ago:

> As children bring their broken toys, with tears for us to mend. I brought my broken dreams to God because he was my friend. But then instead of leaving him in peace to work alone, I hung around and tried to help, with ways that were my own. At last I snatched them back and cried how can you be so slow. "My child," he said, "what could I do, you never did let go." (Author Unknown)

Can you relate to that? We must let go, understanding that we can bring everything in our life to God. This is an important first step because it is impossible to get close to someone who you are constantly pushing away. We must learn to overcome the *I-can-do-it-myself* mentality.

Leave the Light On!

Early in my walk with the Lord, I had a pastor friend who agreed to be my mentor. We met on a regular basis and enjoyed a good cup of coffee and a time of meaningful fellowship. As I was complaining about some of life's challenges one day, I remember him saying, "The problem with you D'Acchioli is that you don't leave the light on."

I replied, "What do you mean by that?"

Then he explained, "Well, we all possess this remote-control light switch, it's called Jesus. We are free to turn it on anytime we want. However, you seem to turn it on only when you are in trouble. You have to leave it on!"

It is funny, I remember thinking this exact same thing during the time of the Gulf War several years ago. Even the most liberal of the news media were on television asking the American people to turn to the Lord in prayer. I am sure that most of them did not even have a true understanding of what that meant; it just seemed like the politically correct thing to do. As a society, we have a habit of turning to God only in times of trouble. You see, we tend to get comfortable in the darkness.

The wise counsel of my pastor friend could not have been simpler, "If you leave the light on, you won't find yourself in as much trouble." Think about it this way. If you were to go home tonight and enter into a completely dark house, you would probably know exactly how to navigate around the obstacles that exist without turning the light switch on. Why? Because you have memorized where the obstacles are.

Now, what if one of your family members decided to move a few things around on you? You would likely enter into a dark room and stumble over those pieces that had been relocated. After your first Dick Van Dyke trip over the ottoman, what would you do? Turn the light on! Illuminate the room! There is no need to stumble your way through the darkness of life. What my pastor friend was really saying is that if you leave the light on, you won't be tripping over stuff! It's the difference between being ready for life's inevitable minefields or wishing you were more prepared after the mishap.

How Do I Begin?

What I am about to share next is not very profound, but once grasped, it has the potential to drastically change your life. Strong friendships are not built easily. They take time. We have to get to know someone inside and out before trusting them enough to confide in them. The same is true of our relationship with God. The only way we can become intimate is by spending time alone with Him.

Time with the Master

Reading the Word, praying, and praising are the three areas I want to emphasize here. I believe we need to have a deliberate scheduled time alone with God every day. We need to develop a devotional habit that will encourage a deeper walk with Him. Coming together as a church on Saturday night or Sunday morning is vital for spiritual growth, but that should never take the place of our private time with God. You cannot develop intimacy in a crowd. It doesn't work. I know because I have tried. I used to convince myself, "I went to church today, I've done my God thing for the week." As a result, I would avoid reading the Word and all of the other things that God was calling me to do. Before long, my relationship with the Lord grew stagnant, and I began to understand the significance of reading the Word, praying, and praising.

You cannot develop intimacy in a crowd.

Reading the Word

Let's dive into these three essential acts a little deeper. I want to begin by looking at some important verses in the Bible. Joshua 1:8 states, "Do not let this book of the law depart from your mouth, meditate on it day and night." Second Timothy 3:16 emphasizes, "All scripture is God-breathed and is useful for teaching, rebuking and training in righteousness so that the man of God may be thoroughly equipped for every good work." In Matthew 22:29, Jesus said, "You are in error because you do not know the scriptures nor the power of God." Romans 15:4 follows, "Everything that was written in the past was written to teach us so that through endurance and the encouragement of the scriptures, we might have hope." In 1 Timothy 4:13 Paul writes, "Until I come, devote yourself to the public reading of scriptures to preaching and teaching."

I have an illustration that exemplifies how many of us like to treat God's Word. I am sure that you have at least one computer sitting in your home. If not, you probably have a basic understanding of how a computer works. The hardware is nothing more than the platform upon which some very sophisticated software programs will run. The real brilliance is in the software. A programmer sits down and writes incredible volumes of code in order to produce a product that you and I will eventually buy at some retail outlet.

However, before this product makes it to the shelf, it goes through an elaborate packaging process. Inside the package, there is usually a pretty healthy size manual. You see, the original writer of the program knew that we would not be able to figure it all out, so he or she provided a manual. Well, if you are anything like me, you don't need to read the instructions. You can figure out how the first 5 to 10 percent of the program works.

In my case, my manual often ends up somewhere on the top shelf of my office right next to my Bible. Until one day, I decide to go a little deeper. I attempt a new command and find myself staring at a blue screen covered with error messages.

What's the first thing I do? I call for technical support. After listening to elevator music for what seems to be an endless length of time, a voice finally answers and our conversation goes something like this:

"Hello, Mr. D'Acchioli. How may I help you?"

"Well, I'm using this program and it just isn't doing what I am asking."

"Well what is it doing, sir?"

" I am asking it to perform a, b, c and it is responding with x, y, z."

"Sir, do you happen to have your manual handy?"

"Yes, hang on a second, and I will pull it down from my bookshelf."

"Okay, now turn to page 974. Do you see the illustration at the top of the page? Is that what your computer is doing?"

"Yes, that is exactly what is happening."

"Do you see the instructions just below that diagram?"

"Yes."

" If you follow the instructions provided right below that illustration, you will avoid having this problem again."

In other words—if you do this, that won't happen.

Feeling rather silly, I quickly thank the technician and hang up the phone. But not before hearing the technician respond, "You are welcome Mr. D'Acchioli. Thank you for calling and have a wonderful day." I am sure that was not what he wanted to say . . .

Do you know what? You also have been manufactured. Just like that computer program, someone wrote your code and knows how every part of your program is supposed to work. Then He plopped you down on planet earth and sent along a manual. That's right, your Bible. God knew that you and I needed more information. But if you are like most people, you don't read that manual. You know how the first 5 to 10 percent of your program works. Most of us are pretty good at figuring out the basic stuff that seems to work in life. Things are looking fine when, all of a sudden, something goes wrong. Your program isn't working like you thought—your marriage is falling apart. What's the first thing you do? You call the technical support department, in this case a pastor or counselor at your church.

"Pastor, something is wrong—there is no way that God gave me that man or that woman—there must be a mistake."

Your pastor responds, "Do you have your manual?"

"What?"

"You know, your Bible."

After digging out the dust-covered Bible, you are asked to turn to Ephesians, the fifth chapter. Fumbling to remember if that was in the Old or New Testament, you finally get there. Once the pastor has guided you to a full understanding of the passage he suggests, "If you do that—your marriage will no longer be a struggle," or better yet, "If you do this, that won't happen."

After thanking your pastor for his time, you hear him reply,

"I appreciate your coming to me for help—glad to be there for you—now go and have a nice day."

But, that's not what he wanted to say . . .

The Bible says in Psalm 119:105, "Your Word is a lamp to my feet and a light for my path." What is that verse suggesting? Literally, *a lamp to my feet* means that it will illuminate my steps every day—one step at a time. We won't be tripping over the minefields of life.

But then there is an even greater promise. The second half of that verse says *a light for my path.* That means not only will the Word illuminate my daily walk, but it will shine a bright light on where I am headed. Want to know why you may be having a hard time discovering the light at the end of your tunnel? I ask you, could it be that you are not in the Word?

Now I understand that reading the Word can be challenging. There have been many times where I have sat down to read two or three chapters in the Bible, and just a few minutes later I cannot remember what I just read. Then there are times when my mind is just too scattered to absorb anything. There are just too many distractions. A friend of mine once warned me, "Don't let the enemy come in and rob you of the truth." He will get you thinking, "Why do I bother reading the Word? I don't get anything out of it." *Read it anyway!*

I am reminded of an old computer saying, "Garbage in—garbage out." We must ask ourselves the question, "What are we putting in?" It only makes sense that what we sow we shall eventually reap, and what we put in will eventually come out. Have you ever had a Scripture verse come to mind that you didn't even remember reading? Read and it will penetrate! Persist and you will reap the benefit!

The Power of Prayer

A second means of becoming more intimate with the Father is through prayer. Prayer must become a significant part of our devotional habit. *When* you decide to set apart the time is not as important as the *quality* of time spent. Mornings have always been the best opportunity for me to spend time alone with God.

I would like to share with you what I like to call, "The Six Principles for Effective Prayer:"

1. Schedule It

If you don't schedule it, you won't do it. I read a book many years ago titled, *Eckerd.* It was an autobiography of Jack Eckerd's life. Jack was the founder of a large and very successful drug store chain. In his book, he talks about how he would go to work every morning and retreat directly to his office. Each day from 7:30 A.M. to roughly 8:30 A.M. he closed his office door and shut the rest of the world out. His first meeting of the day was scheduled with God. Jack's secretary was aware that this meeting was more important than any board meeting or conference call that might attempt to interrupt him and she did her best to insure that he was never disturbed. Jack protected that time as though it was the most precious meeting in the work place. What a great example of how we should be treating our intimate moments with the Father.

2. Find a Quiet Place

This may be your office, a study, your basement or a place in your home where there is little family traffic. Some people have even designated a special room or closet in their home especially for the purpose of prayer. Wherever it may be, be sure to create a private prayer haven of your very own. If you don't have a quiet place, you will never be able to achieve number three . . .

3. Quiet Your Mind

This is the greatest challenge for me. It is tough to get my mind into a place of neutral where I am not thinking about anything else but God. To get there, I generally start by praising Him. I may say something like, "Lord I love you, I give you honor, glory and praise. You are such a wonderful God." Just begin to talk to Him as if He were sitting right at your side. Thank Him and honor Him. Before you know it, everything that was previously clouding your thoughts will fall away and your focus will be on Jesus alone.

4. Seek Him First—Not What You Want

If your mind is quiet and you are truly operating with a heart of praise, it will only be natural to seek God's face rather than His hand. I do not mean to say that it is wrong to bring our petitions before the Lord. The Word clearly instructs us to cast all of our cares on Him. However, it is important that we learn to seek the Giver of the gift before we seek the gift. We are so quick to jump right in with our requests. Can you imagine how a loving parent would feel if the only time their child ever came to them was when he or she wanted something? Should our Father God feel any different? He loves us and desires to spend quality time with us. First seek . . . then ask!

5. Ask for His Will in All Matters

His plan is perfect and right for every circumstance. In Mark 14:36 Jesus states, "Father everything is possible for You. Take this cup from me." In this verse, Jesus is referring to His pending death on the cross. He continues, "Yet not what I will, but what You will." Even though He knew what was about to happen, He was willing to endure it in order to see God's will fulfilled.

6. Pray against the Forces That Oppose God's Will

As a result of Jesus' death on the cross, and His shed blood, you and I have been given the authority to pray against all forces that are at cross purposes with God's will. What are those forces? There are three: The world, the flesh, and the devil. If we pray for God's will we should never be disappointed with the outcome. We can rejoice knowing that He will answer our petition in His own way and in His own time.

Giving Him Praise

It is funny how we sing about praise, we talk about it and we even use it in our spiritual lingo, "Praise the Lord!" But how many of us have established a habit of personal praise? Did you realize that the word praise is mentioned 319 times in the Bible? It is one of the most often mentioned concepts in all of Scripture, yet one of the most misunderstood. Most of us do not understand what praise really means.

About twenty-five years ago when I was a new believer, the concept of praise came to rest with me. It was a significant event in my life. God spoke to me. While it was not in an audible voice, I knew beyond a shadow of a doubt that it was Him. At the time, Cindy and I had been married for almost fifteen years. We were attending a marriage retreat together. We were seated in the back of the room so that I could run the sound booth. Cindy was positioned in the last pew, and I was standing behind her, trying to gently ease some of the tension out of her neck. As this was taking place, the pastor began to preach about the necessity for husbands and wives to encourage each other more often. He said, "For every time a positive word is spoken, there are eleven negative words spoken."

Upon hearing this, I remember thinking, "That's right. You know Cindy doesn't encourage me enough. I hope she is listening to this!" I was completely riled up. The irony of it all is that I did not deserve much encouragement in those days. Even so, I continued to complain to God, "I hope You are convicting Cindy's heart. She never encourages me and I need encouragement. She never lifts me up. She never praises me." As soon as I finished that last thought, I heard God say, "I know the feeling." Those four little words hit me like a dagger. He continued, "Get your eyes off of Cindy and begin to praise me." Wow! I'd like to tell you that my whole idea of praise changed after that experience. It didn't. It took years to develop a habit of praise and I am still working on it.

Over time, I have learned that God's voice is always heard the clearest during moments of intense praise. Second Chronicles 5:13 states, "The trumpeters and singers joined in unison as with one voice to give praise and thanks to the Lord. Accompanied by trumpets, symbols, and other instruments they raised their voices in praise to the Lord and sang, He is good, His love endures forever." The verse continues, "Then, (then is a transitional word meaning as a result of what has just taken place, here is what happened) the temple of the Lord was filled with a cloud." The cloud, of course, was God's presence. Under the Old Covenant, God would reside in physical locations—the Temple, Tabernacle, or Ark.

Under the New Covenant, 2 Chronicles 5:13 has a whole different connotation. Where does God reside today? That's right, in our hearts. Wow, what a promise. As the direct result of praising our God, He blesses us with His very presence. Scripture tells us that the Lord inhabits the praises of His people.

As Precious As a Puppy

Several years ago, Cindy and I had the joy of bringing home a brand new Golden Retriever puppy named Katie. Her arrival came during a very challenging time in my life. I was searching for God's direction regarding the founding of my own ministry to men. The thought of leaving a meaningful corporate position with all of the attending satisfaction and financial security was a scary one. I had grown accustomed to those regular paychecks. Where I was thinking of heading I knew a steady income would no longer be a guarantee. With mixed emotion I began to seek the Lord for guidance.

I will never forget one particular morning when I was calling out to the Lord in the solitude of our basement. At the time, little Katie had only been with us for a few days. She loved to follow me around, and that day she was wandering around the basement as I prayed. I remember standing by the back door saying, "Lord, I just love you, I just praise you. You're such a good God." Suddenly I felt a warm impression on my left foot. As I looked down I saw that Katie had positioned herself on my slipper and was looking up at me with those irresistible puppy dog eyes. I began to cry as I heard God whisper in my ear, "How does that feel?" It felt wonderful! Katie just wanted to be close to me. She wanted me to pet her. She was lying on a foot that could literally crush her. But that did not matter—she just wanted to cuddle. Then the Lord spoke to me again and said, "Vince, that doesn't even come close to how I feel when you do that with Me." I broke into an even more intense time of weeping. I know that those thoughts could have never come from my own mind. I knew that I had heard from God. What a tender and powerful moment that was!

It is difficult to comprehend the extent to which God loves us and desires to be close to us. While my story about Katie may seem a bit silly, it represents yet another intimate moment with the Father. Most of us know what it is like to hold and cuddle a small baby in our arms. What a feeling that is when that small wonder clings to you and hugs you back! God longs to have the very same relationship with us.

If You Praise Him—He Will Speak!

I would like to suggest that there is a direct link between praising God and hearing His voice. James 4:8 says, "Come near to God and He will come near to you." Are you tuned to the Master's voice? Is His hand in your glove?

One day when Katie was about six months old, she was out wandering in our front yard. She was running around enjoying the scents and freedom of the great outdoors. When I came out to check on her, I noticed that my neighbor was just getting into her car to leave. I was concerned that Katie would run into her path and began to call her home. There was no response. She was too busy sniffing life. I continued to yell, "Katie come! Danger! Get out of there!"

How many times does God try to deliver that same warning message to us? Yet we never hear Him because we are too busy "sniffing life!" That day in the yard, I was forced to go and grab Katie in order to get her attention. More often than not, that is what God has to do with us. Or sadly, He sometimes allows us to get run over.

Today Katie is seven years old. Now when I call her, she comes almost immediately and sits at my feet. Why? What is the difference between that six-month old puppy and this seven-year-old dog? She is tuned to her master's voice. How did that happen? We talked about it earlier. It's that four-letter word that so scares us: t-i-m-e. We spent time together. My friend, you will never be tuned to the Master's voice until you spend time with the Master.

Three Sets of Four Words

There is one final story that I would like to share with you before concluding this chapter. Several years ago, I drove up to the mountains by myself to fast and pray for my wife. I had just left my position as vice-president for a Fortune 1000 company to enter into ministry. My new job required that Cindy and I leave our home in California and relocate to Colorado Springs, Colorado. In doing so, we left behind our home (the home that Cindy had originally grown up in), all of our relatives, and an abundance of dear friends.

Upon arriving in Colorado we immediately took on the overwhelming project of building a new house. Are you tired yet? The story gets better! Shortly after we settled into our new place, our daughter Kimberly decided to surprise us with the news of her engagement. Within a very short time, we had experienced a major career change, a relocation, the task of building a new home, and the planning of a wedding! The impact was devastating to Cindy, and she was left emotionally drained. This is when I decided to retreat to the mountains to fast and pray for three days on her behalf.

My first day up at that cabin was miserable. My room was void of any modern conveniences. There was no phone and no television. After unpacking, I began to pray and ask the Lord to speak to me. I was disappointed when there was no response. That entire first day God did not communicate one thing to me. I was starting to get discouraged. I felt spiritually dry.

It was not until midway through the second day that I began to hear God's voice. What He spoke was delivered to me in three sets of four words. I immediately knew that it was Him. As I continued to pray for Cindy, I received the first set of words. God said to tell Cindy, *"I love you, Cindy."* I must admit that I was a bit disappointed. That seemed too simple. I was ready to jot down some profound theological point with fourteen sub-points!

As I began to pray again, the Lord spoke to me a second time. He instructed me to tell Cindy, *"My plans are good."*

"Okay Lord that is nice, but when are you going to give me some real meat? Your Word tells me that your plans are for good and not for evil that we might have a future and a hope. I'm looking for some new material here." I was actually quoting Bible verses to God!

After another hour had passed; I received the last set of four words. The Lord said to tell Cindy, *"Stay close to me."* That was it. He was done talking. The next day came and was as spiritually dry as the first. I had invested three days in fasting and prayer for three simple sets of four words. I felt like a failure as I drove home with those twelve little words on a small notepad. What was I going to tell Cindy? I was sure that she was expecting so much more.

Still whining, I pulled into the driveway and Cindy immediately came bolting out of the door into the garage. She seemed so happy to see me, "Welcome home! she said. "I've had the most wonderful time with God over the last three days. I can't wait to hear what God has said to you." I started to feel my stomach knot up as I thought about how I was going to milk these three sets of four words. Eventually, I pulled the small sheet of notepaper from my pocket and began to read what the Lord had shared. As I did, Cindy began to cry. "Was it something I said?" Most of us guys are clueless when our wives cry—we don't know what's going on. Then the most amazing thing happened. Through her tears Cindy said, "That is the most fantastic thing I have ever heard. That is exactly what God shared with me. He directed me to it in the Word." Wow! I went from a zero to a hero in just a matter of seconds!

The following week I was invited to speak at a staff chapel for a large ministry in Colorado Springs. My audience was primarily made up of Evangelical Christians. For about forty-five minutes I delivered a teaching that was based on the three sets of four words that I just shared. By the time I was done speaking, people were weeping all around the room. How could such a simple message penetrate the hearts of so many? God's message for us is not complicated. In spite of their simplicity, twelve words can have a profound impact.

Here is what I believe God is trying to tell you and me right now:

I don't care what your friends think about you.

I don't care what your neighbors think about you.

I don't care what the people at work think about you.

I don't care what your family or the people in your church think about you.

In fact, I don't even care what you think about you.

I LOVE YOU! With a love that goes so far beyond anything you can comprehend. You are precious in my sight.

WOW! I do not know how God can love us like that—but He does.

Then He says this:

I don't care where you've been or what you've done.

Yes, I know about that dirty magazine—those drugs.

I know about how you are thinking about the man or woman at work.

I know about the affair—the failures.

I know how broken you think you are.

But, I sent my Son Jesus to die on a cross for you and to once and for all draw a line in the sand that separates you from your past.

MY PLANS ARE GOOD!

And guess when God's plan for your life begins? Right now—this very second. It is not hindered in any way because of your past. Have we messed up along the way? Sure we have—but isn't it great to know that we have a God of fresh starts?

Finally, He wants you to know that the secret to understanding how an invisible God can love you like He does and the key to discovering His wonderful plan for your life lies in that third set of four words,

STAY CLOSE TO ME!

My friend, please hear me. God loves you and wants to reveal *how* and *why* He made you. As I said earlier, you will never discover God's plan for your life unless you are willing to get close to Him. Here is the winning formula: *Intimacy with God = Strength of Vision.*

Can It Be True?

Lamentations 3:22-23 is where Jeremiah is looking over the rubble of a destroyed city. Many of us, like Jeremiah, might be in a similar place looking over what we think is the rubble of a destroyed life. Consider what Jeremiah says, "Because of the Lord's great love we are not consumed, for His compassions never fail. They are new every morning . . ."

Just like the rebuilding of a destroyed city, God can rebuild our lives. The key is getting close to the Builder. If you have already accepted Jesus as your Lord and Savior, make a commitment right now to get closer to Him. If you have not, perhaps you are still searching—doubting. You are wondering, can all this be true—it sounds too good. The answer is *yes*. God is real and He loves you beyond anything you can think or imagine. Accept Him now. Before going any further in this book, just ask Him to come into your heart. He will, and you will never be the same.

Chapter Summary:

1. The only way to overcome the hurt and pain associated with a dysfunctional relationship with your earthly father is to establish an intimate relationship with your Heavenly One.

2. We will never get to know and trust God unless we spend time alone with Him.

3. In order to truly know God you must practice three things: Read the Word—pray—and praise Him. Combine all three and take a daily dose!

4. There is a powerful relationship between praising God and hearing His voice.

Discussion Questions:

1. On a scale of one to ten (ten being the highest and best), how would I rate my relationship with God?

2. What specific things can I begin to do today to move up on the scale?

Write down one or two key ideas that you gleaned from this chapter and at least one new behavior you would like to start practicing.

Key Ideas

___

___

___

___

New Behavior/Commitment

___

___

___

___

Coming Up in Chapter Three:

We begin the process of discovering *how* and *why* God made you. In this powerful chapter you will learn all about your natural areas of giftedness. You will also discover how these gifts affect the way you view life and make decisions. Be prepared to take the *Natural Gift Test* and discover the vocational implications.

Chapter Three

How I Am Wired

The "Peter Principle"

The Fortune 1000 company that I worked for had 150 retail locations. I was responsible for two to three thousand employees who worked in those stores. Therefore, most approvals for the position of store manager crossed my desk.

For the sake of privacy, I will refer to this gentleman as Dennis. He was the assistant manager of one of our most profitable and well-run stores. He consistently received high marks in all the important areas of operation, customer service, merchandising and training ability. When the time came to consider him for a promotion to store manager, it was an easy decision.

A year later, we had to let Dennis go. As a store manager, he was failing in almost every area where he had once received the highest marks. Why? How could this high achiever be so good as an assistant and fail as a manager? In the business world, we call this the "Peter Principle," promoting someone beyond his or her level of ability. Most often, it is not the employees' fault. Rather, it is management's inability to properly assess their *natural gifts*. That was the case with Dennis. All of us who knew him had failed to recognize that Dennis was a great number two man, but would easily crumble under the pressures associated with the top spot. Tell him what to do—he was great. Turn him loose to make his own judgments—he would fail.

Although I was familiar with this principle, I had not done enough homework on this particular promotion. I had not asked the right questions—subjected him to enough testing. This taught me an important lesson. I learned that each and every person is gifted in special ways. I learned that sometimes the worst thing we can do is to ask someone to do a job for which they are ill equipped, or that is beyond their area of expertise. I have also learned that it is not fair to judge people on the basis of their performance too prematurely. I believe that we live in a society where a lot of round pegs are trying to fill square holes. That is why I am not surprised by a recent statistic that indicates that two out of every three people are discontent at work.

To what can we attribute this? Allow me to suggest two contributing factors. First, we live in a world that places progressive values on various careers. By that I mean, if you are a bank president, people tend to think more highly of you than if you are a bank teller. One of the most dramatic indicators of this is the way our culture has turned perhaps the most important responsibility in life, caring for children in the home, into a low-level job. Today, if you are a stay-at-home mom or dad, you are often considered a second-class citizen. You should get a real job, look out for yourself. After all, who else will? Most of this has happened as the direct result of greed born out of a materialistic and selfish society.

While this is a serious problem that demands a solution, I would like to change my focus to what I believe is the second contributing factor, which has to do with not understanding our natural areas of giftedness. It is obvious that we have each been built differently. We all have unique gifts and talents which, when exercised in the right way, can bring about great fulfillment. That is what this chapter is all about, discovering *how* we are built or *wired.*

I would like to pause here in order to bring a context to this discussion by returning to something that was touched on earlier in my introduction.

The Three Unalterable Facts

What I am going to share with you now has become the foundation for my life, my ministry and this book. I call it the *Three Unalterable Facts:*

Fact #1: God knows you and has created you for a special purpose.
Fact #2: God has given you special gifts toward the satisfaction of His purpose.
Fact #3: God wants you to discover what His purpose is.

Let's take a look at each fact individually . . .

Fact #1: God knows you and has created you for a special purpose.

The Bible says in Jeremiah 1:5, "Before I formed you in the womb I knew you, before you were born I set you apart; I appointed you as a prophet to the nations." Of course we know that this is God speaking to Jeremiah. We need to understand that God wants to say this to everyone who calls upon Him. That means you and me. If that is not enough to convince you, then take a look at some of these verses:

Isaiah 44:2 "This is what the Lord says—he who made you, who formed you in the womb, and who will help you. . . ."

Psalm 139:13-17 "For you created my inmost being; you knit me together in my mother's womb. I praise you because I am fearfully and wonderfully made; your works are wonderful, I know that full well. My frame was not hidden from you when I was made in the secret place. When I was woven together in the depths of the earth, your eyes saw my unformed body. All the days ordained for me were written in your book before one of them came to be."

Ephesians 1:11 "In him we were also chosen, having been predestined according to the plan of him who works out everything in conformity with the purpose of his will." (I call this the real planned parenthood—His plan.)

Ephesians 2:10 "For we are God's workmanship, created in Christ Jesus to do good works, which God prepared in advance for us to do . . ."

Proverbs 23:18 "There is surely a future hope for you, and your hope will not be cut off . . ."

Jeremiah 29:11 "For I know the plans I have for you," declares the Lord, "plans to prosper you and not to harm you, plans to give you hope and a future . . ."

Fact #2: God has given you special gifts toward the satisfaction of His purpose.

Romans 12:4-6 says, "Just as each of us has one body with many members, and these members do not all have the same function, so in Christ we who are many form one body, and each member belongs to all the others. We have different gifts, according to the grace given us . . ."

These are the gifts that we will be covering in this chapter. The Bible makes it clear that we are not all the same. We have different gifts—or temperaments—designed to assist us with our assigned task. Look at what it says in 1 Peter 4:10,

"Each one should use whatever gift he has received to serve others, faithfully administering God's grace in its various forms . . ."

Fact #3: God wants you to discover what His purpose is.

Ephesians 1:18 states, "I pray also that the eyes of your heart may be enlightened in order that you may know the hope to which he has called you, the riches of his glorious inheritance in the saints . . ."

God has called you for a special purpose. He has a plan or *vision* for your life. The next chapter is devoted to this last unalterable fact. For now, I want to deal with number two, our natural gifts.

Our Natural Gifts

When we talk about the study of human behavior, there are a number of terms we use to define our different personalities. You may have heard terms like characteristics, natural gifts, motivational gifts, talents, temperaments, etc. You have probably also noticed a plethora of testing instruments which attempt to help you discover your particular gift or bent. I have personally taken just about every test available and have found that, for the most part, they are all pretty accurate with slight variations. If you are a Christian, you have probably taken at least one of the many spiritual gift tests that are out there. These, too, can be very helpful, but in my view, tend to blur the lines between our natural makeup and God's impartation of special or unique gifts.

While there are a lot of good gift and temperament analysis devices out there, I want to focus on the one I have found to be the best. It's right out of the Bible. In fact, it can be found in the book of Romans, the twelfth chapter. Before turning to this scripture, I would like to talk about spiritual gifts in a broader sense. In the Bible, at least three categories of gifts are referred to. Let me relate a teaching I heard once that might bring some clarity to this discussion.

The first category, often referred to as the *spiritual* or *power* gifts, can be found in 1 Corinthians 12:8-10. These are the gifts that are somewhat controversial within the church today. Because they deal with miracles and signs and wonders, there are some that doubt they still exist. Others believe that they are alive and well. Let me say at the outset that these are not the gifts we will be concentrating on.

The second category, called *ministry* or *service* gifts can be found in Ephesians 4:11-12 and 1 Corinthians 12:28. Some believe that if in the first instance the power gifts are given by the Holy Spirit for miracles, signs and wonders—that these ministry gifts are given by Jesus himself for service within the church. For the purpose of our study, we will not be referring to this category either.

What I want to do is concentrate on the third category, sometimes referred to as the seven *natural, persona, motivational,* or *charismata* gifts. These gifts are found in Romans 12:6-8. I believe that these gifts are not genetic or hereditary. They are given by the Father Himself and represent our natural temperament or bent. I am also convinced that with rare exception these gifts or temperaments do not change. These gifts will stay much the same throughout your life.

Let's look at Romans 12:6-8:

> We have different gifts, according to the grace given us. If a man's gift is prophesying, let him use it in proportion to his faith. If it is serving, let him serve; if it is teaching, let him teach; if it is encouraging, let him encourage; if it is contributing to the needs of others, let him give generously; if it is leadership, let him govern diligently; if it is showing mercy, let him do it cheerfully.

These verses talk about seven distinct gifts: *prophesying, serving, teaching, encouraging, contributing, leadership,* and *mercy.* Some of the gifts that I have just named are referred to differently, depending upon the biblical translation or particular gift test. For instance, *prophesying* could also be *perceiving.* This does not mean prophecy in the sense of foretelling something. Rather it suggests perception—a perceptive person. *Serving* is sometimes called *ministry. Encouraging* could be *exhorting. Contributing* might be *giving. Leadership* could be *administration,* and so on . . .

Here is an important idea and the reason why this chapter is so critical. I am convinced that all of us possess one or more of these gifts. I have also discovered that we will make decisions and view life through the filtering system associated with our gift. In other words, our gifts become a paradigm through which we live our lives. This often occurs unconsciously. Later on, we will study the behavioral characteristics associated with your gifts, and you will begin to understand why this is so crucial to your appreciation of others, and to your discovering the ultimate purpose for your life.

From the Very Beginning

In the book of Proverbs, the Bible tells us that we should train up a child in the way he should go. An honest study of that verse reveals something very different than what might be gleaned from a casual reading. It literally means that mom and dad need to study their child, determine how God has built him or her uniquely, and train up that child in *that* way. I am convinced that you can see evidence of how God designed a person from his or her infancy.

At the risk of taking off on a few grandpa stories, let me just share one experience we had with our new grandson, Parker. Before he was even 1-year-old, he completely took apart a complicated toy and proceeded to swallow the small battery. He continually amazes us when it comes to figuring things out. He is also a great copycat. He only needs to see something once and he has it. Parker is definitely a *perceiver teacher.*

The fact of the matter is that not all babies are like Parker. Some are less active and aware. This is not to suggest anything negative at all—there are positives and negatives associated with every area of giftedness. I am merely suggesting the importance of discovering *how* our little ones have been designed so that we can train them up in *that* way.

Most of us have never been exposed to that kind of guidance and training. While our moms and dads probably wanted to help us grow in positive ways, little attention was usually given to our natural gifts or temperaments. The result of this is that most of us go through life without a full understanding of our natural gifts. Now for the critical question, how does one discover his or her natural gifts?

The Pathway to Discovery

As a Christian, I believe that everything starts with prayer. If we accept the premise that it is God who knows us best and has built us uniquely, then who else can better answer our questions? So, if you are serious about getting the answer to this important question, "Lord *how* did you wire me uniquely?" then I am going to suggest three things for you to do (the first is the most critical):

1. Pray

Go before God every day until you get an answer. Just ask Him, "Lord, please help me to better understand how You made me. When You look at me Lord, what do You see?" Once you have done this you can now move to the second thing.

2. Go On a Treasure Hunt

Start talking to people who know you. Ask them what they think your strong and weak points are. Sometimes you can get some very helpful insights in this way.

Let me share something I did several years ago while on my personal journey to know *how* God made me. I made a list of a number of people in my life who knew me best. They included my wife and kids, pastor, co-workers, my CEO at work, and others. Some were Christian—some were not. That doesn't matter to God—He can speak through anyone. After I made the list, I began to schedule interviews with all of these people. I started with my family. The question was the same for everyone, "What do you think are my natural gifts—what about my obvious weaknesses?" Keep in mind here that this is a wonderful exercise, but if you are serious about doing it, you need to be prepared for the consequences.

I find that people are eager to tell you what they think. Some have been anxiously awaiting the opportunity. I took advantage of this by writing down what people said and before long I was able to see a pattern that made sense. It was an eye-opening exercise.

I remember having lunch one day with a man named Dick. Dick was attending a marriage class that Cindy and I had been teaching for several years. I asked him why he attended and what was he hearing that kept him coming back? He shared information that really helped me better understand my message and approach to teaching, information that has been invaluable over the years.

3. Take a Natural Gifts Test

A word of caution here! There are a lot of good testing instruments out there. Many of them tend to take all of the gifts that are referred to in the Bible and lump them together. I find those tests to be too voluminous and at times, confusing. I prefer sticking to the natural gifts or temperament-oriented tests. These more closely reflect your natural instincts and will better help you understand how you think and make decisions in life.

In the Appendix of this book, I have included a simple test, one which, over the years has proven to be very accurate. Before you read any further, I want to recommend that you stop and take this test. It will require about thirty minutes of your time and will make the rest of our discussion about this subject more meaningful. This test is a condensed version of several other high quality devices. In giving this test to thousands of men and women over the years, I have found it to be very helpful. I might also add that if you are a pastor, business leader, or have the responsibility of supervising others, this can be a valuable tool for helping place people in the right position or giving them assignments that take full advantage of their gifts.

You may want to photocopy the test pages so that you can administer it again to family and friends. This same test and additional information for further study can be found on our web site at www.otm.org. This topic is also covered in excellent detail in a book titled, *Understanding Your God Given Gifts*, written by Don and Katie Fortune.

Please take the time to fill out the test before continuing with this chapter.

Making the Grade

Now that you have taken the test, let's debrief you on the results. You have just rated whether or not a given list of behavioral characteristics applied to you. Those characteristics were broken into seven categories representing the seven natural gifts. Upon totaling your points, you probably discovered that you have a couple of areas where you scored higher. Highlight those top two categories. These two areas reflect *how* God has wired you.

In almost every case, this test will pinpoint two dominant sets of characteristics. However, on occasion, I have found that some people end up with three or four that are too close to call. If this happens, I suggest that you go back, retake the test, and think through each statement more thoroughly. This should help clarify the outcome.

The best way to get a quick understanding of the result is to review the list of characteristics where you scored the highest. In essence, you are reading a description of yourself. In other words, these are your behavioral characteristics. You can already see some powerful information about yourself that should help you better understand why you react to situations and make certain decisions.

I want to suggest that while these gifts are all unique in and of themselves, there are at least two categories that can be loosely defined. These are what I call the soft-sided and hard-sided gifts. *Ministry, exhorting, giving* and *mercy* tend to be the soft-sided gifts while *perceiver, teaching,* and *administration* lean toward the hard side. Soft-sided people tend to be more sensitive to others' needs, patient, and anxious to help. The down side can be a lack of organization and an inability to apply logical and structured thought. Hard-sided people tend to be good at organization, logical and structured, but not always as sensitive to other's needs. I realize that this is a broad brush. I will provide more details on this later.

Again, I am not suggesting that one side is more favorable than the other. We must remember that God says they are all good and necessary. How we use them in life to compliment one another is the key. Let me share an experience I had while administering this test to a large group of married couples. I began by telling them a story—setting up a hypothetical scene. It went like this:

> You and your spouse are in a supermarket shopping, when down an aisle you spot Johnny. You don't know him very well—you think he is about 12-years-old or so. He just moved into your neighborhood with his mom and dad last month. From the looks of their yard and the car that they drive, you make an assumption that they do not have a lot of money. They seem friendly enough—waving when they walk by and so forth—but that is all you know.
>
> Little Johnny does not see you, but you see him. He is looking rather suspicious. At one point you see him reach for an item on the shelf and put it into his pocket. Later you see him leaving the store without having paid for the item.

When I finished telling the story I asked my audience, "What would you do?" The response was immediate and quite comical. One man raised his hand and said, "I'd turn him in."

His wife, sitting next to him suddenly bent her arm and gave him a swift blow to his side with her elbow. "You'd what?" she replied.

After his shock, he then said, "I'd turn him in—why—what would you do?"

"Why, I'd pray for him," she replied.

"Pray for him, give me a break," the man replied. That exchange initiated a tremendous response from my audience. In fact, I heard over thirty different responses for the same situation.

Why is this? I believe that we react to situations and make decisions based upon the filtering system associated with our natural gifts. What I did after we recorded all of the responses was to go over to the white board and neatly place all of them under the headings of the seven gifts. My audience was then able to see that their reaction was typical of someone who possesses that gift.

Here is where we can get into trouble. Let's say that I have just witnessed this scene with little Johnny and am looking for some ideas on what to do. In seeking an answer I go to Mark, who has a strong *teaching* gift. Mark's response might be something like, "Well, I guess I would come up with a plan—maybe involve the parents, store manager and even find a police officer who might help. I would try to confront the boy and create an experience he would never forget." Okay advice I suppose, but not exactly what I am looking for.

Next, I turn to my friend Pete, "Hey Pete, what would you do?" Having the gift of *ministry* or *mercy* Pete suggests, "I guess I would probably just buy him a bag of groceries—maybe try to get to know the family—I would be sure to pray for them." In total disagreement, I decide to move on to Mary.

Mary has the gifts of *perceiver* and *administration.* Her gifts just happen to be more like mine. "Mary, what would you do?" She responds, "I'd turn him in, in a New York second." All right! Finally an answer that I agree with! I reach up and give Mary a big high five.

What just happened with Mark, Pete, and Mary? I simply moved from one to the next until I found the one with the same gift filtering system as I had, someone who would tell me exactly what *I* wanted to hear. Rather than allowing our various gifts to complement each other, we sometimes beat each other up with them. That is why understanding *how* we are wired is so important.

It has taken us a long time, but Cindy and I have finally learned that we need to defer to one another in certain situations, depending upon the way God made us. We are very different. She is definitely more toward the soft side than I am. I know that there are times where my response is not what is needed and have learned how precious her input is. After all, God gave her that. I have also found numerous occasions where husbands and wives will score high in the same areas. This can be reason for joy—obviously they will both look at situations and challenges in much the same way. In this case however, I strongly recommend that they do not make important life decisions alone. Often, we need the perspective of those who may approach that situation through different eyes. It is helpful to add their input to the decision making process in order to gain a more well rounded view.

There is one more subtlety I need to mention here. The reason why I am asking you to look at your two highest scores is that your second gift can have a profound impact on your first. For example, let's assume that someone has the gift of *giving*. This is a wonderful gift and you know you have it when you find yourself giving of your time or money and never having to be recognized for it. Some people have this as their primary gift and their next highest might be *mercy* or *ministry*. Others might have gifts like *administration* or *perceiver* as their secondary gift. Here is the not-so-subtle difference . . .

In the first case, you would likely be someone who would freely give of your money and time—it would give you great pleasure—but you would not necessarily need to be intimately connected to the recipient. In the latter case you would give—feel just as satisfied—but you would want an accounting. You would want to know where the money or effort was going and how much of a difference it was going to make. You can see here that we have the same primary gift—administered in a very different way because of the influence of the secondary gift.

A Word of Caution

Your gifts are NOT a license for you to be the way they say you are! Wow, what a mouthful. Here is what I mean. "Well Cindy, the reason why I am a little cold and calculating at times—overly short and impatient is because that's the way God built me—you're just going to have to live with it." Whoa! Or maybe it is Cindy coming to me with, "Well honey, I know that I am sometimes a little late—and not always as organized as you would like—but that is just the way God built me—I guess there is nothing that can be done." Danger!

Please hear me. The Bible is our standard. The Bible says that we must be kind and compassionate to one another, quick to forgive and so on. The Bible also suggests that we be shrewd and count the cost. All this means is that depending upon which side of the natural gift spectrum you may be coming from, it will be harder for you to live up to *the* standard. It does not mean you ignore *the* standard. Your gift, or bent, is not an excuse. It is simply the way you are wired.

Vocational Confusion

I want to conclude this chapter by touching on an important issue. I call it vocational confusion and it happens a lot with people who do not understand how to separate their learned disciplines from their natural gifts. The best way to explain this is to tell you what happened in my life.

As you now know from my story, I came up the ranks of a high profile company and ended up as an administrative vice-president. Because of this, when I began to learn about gifts, I quite obviously thought I had the gift of *administration.* There was a problem, though. I was frustrated and did not know why. It wasn't until I discovered that my real gifts were not administration, but more in the *perceiver teacher* area, that I found my way. You see, my learned discipline (in this case, administration), had suffocated my natural gifts. It wasn't until I found a vent for my natural gifts that I felt real fulfillment.

What happened was that I began to teach and speak more in business settings. I found myself becoming very satisfied as I had more and more invitations to speak on management and leadership issues. What I am saying here is that your natural gift is not necessarily an indication of what you may choose vocationally. However, you are likely to approach whatever vocation you choose through this prism or paradigm. Here is another way of looking at it . . .

Let's look at a pastor of a church who has the gift of *teaching*. In that church, you will likely have strong biblical exegesis coming from the pulpit—highly organized and structured. Now let's put another pastor in the same church with the gift of *administration.* You would probably see more programs and activities—a lot of organizational type meetings, etc. Now let's substitute another pastor with the gift of *ministry* or *mercy.* The result would no doubt be a lot of outreach to the community—hospital visitations—overseas mission trips, etc. Same church—different leaders—different gifts.

I mentioned earlier that your natural gifts are not necessarily an indication of what vocation you might choose. You can be happy wherever you are if you find a vent for your natural gifts. However, if you are in the fortunate position of selecting a future vocation, I believe this information could be very helpful. Now that you know these things about yourself, you have a much better chance of finding a life work that will fill the dual purpose of providing income and optimizing what God has given you.

At the end of the gift test in the Appendix of this book, I have provided a subjective list of potential vocations that correspond to the seven natural gifts. I would encourage you to consider them if you are in the process of searching. If you have already chosen a career path and find that your gift and vocation are a disastrous mismatch, read on! We will address this issue in the next chapter when we discuss *why* God has made you and how you can discover His unique plan for your life.

Until you are sure of God's direction, I recommend that you find a vent for your gift. If you are bent toward *ministry* or *mercy*—volunteer for a mission trip or go on some hospital visitations. If you are more on the *administration* or *teaching* side—start a small-group or Bible study—take on a project, etc. Sometimes as you exercise your gift, God reveals a lot about His future plan for your life.

As a Final Thought—Meditate on These Verses:

Psalm 138:8 "The LORD will fulfill [His purpose] for me; your love, O LORD, endures forever—do not abandon the works of your hands."

Jeremiah 31:17 "So there is hope for your future, declares the LORD."

Philippians 1:6 "Being confident of this, that He who began a good work in you will carry it on to completion until the day of Christ Jesus."

Chapter Summary:

1. Remember the Three Unalterable Facts.

   Fact #1: God knows you and has created you for a special purpose.

Fact #2: God has given you special gifts toward the satisfaction of His purpose.

Fact #3: God wants you to discover what His purpose is.

2. Our natural gifts are the paradigm or filter through which we view life and make decisions.
3. There are three ways to discover *how* God has wired you:
   1. Pray—ask God every day to reveal *how* He made you.
   2. Go on that treasure hunt—ask those close to you what they see.
   3. Take the Natural Gift Test—then find a way to exercise your gifts.
4. Remember that your gifts are not a license to be the way they say you are. Our standard must always be the Word of God.

Discussion Questions:

1. How can I apply my gifts more appropriately at home, in my work, church and community?
2. Think and verbalize one example in your life where not understanding your natural bent has caused a problem.

Write down one or two key ideas that you gleaned from this chapter and at least one new behavior you would like to start practicing.

Key Ideas

____

____

____

____

New Behavior/Commitment

____

____

____

____

Coming Up in Chapter Four:

Learn the importance of *vision* as it relates to focusing your life. Specifically, you will discover the four things that need to line up before you can be certain it is the right direction for you to go.

Chapter Four

Why Am I Here? Discovering God's Plan for Your Life

Losing Your First Love

In the mid eighties, while on the secular speaking circuit, I met a woman by the name of Betsy Sanders. Betsy, in her late thirties at the time, had worked her way up from a sales associate to executive vice-president for Nordstrom Department Stores in the Pacific Northwest.

Betsy told a story at an event I attended that so caught my attention that I asked her if she would come to my company and share it with our executive team. She agreed and this is the story she told:

One day a group of executives from Nordstrom invited a number of top executives from J.C. Penney to a luncheon. They were all seated around a large table enjoying their meal when one of the executives from J.C. Penney asked the following question: "To what do you attribute your tremendous success? Nordstrom has become a model that people all over the world are studying." What he was basically looking for was the key to their success.

The way I remember Betsy telling it, one of the executives from Nordstrom excused himself for a few moments in order to retrieve a large book from an adjacent room. He brought the book over to the Penney's executive, opened it and laid it in front of him. The book, written one hundred years before, was the original operational manual for J.C. Penney.

He simply said, "We do everything that it says in this book."

What an uncomfortable moment that must have been for that team from J.C. Penney. You see, what the executive from Nordstrom was really trying to communicate was that J.C. Penney had lost their first love. They had the *vision* and somewhere along the way they allowed it to slip away. Sadly, this is what happens in the lives of many organizations, churches, marriages, and individuals.

If you do not know where you are going . . .
any road will take you there.

The Bible says in Proverbs, "Where there is no *vision* . . . the people perish." I like the NIV version that states, "Where there is no *revelation* . . . the people cast off restraint." In other words, if you do not know where you are going . . . any road will take you there.

Where are you going?

As a senior executive, I had the opportunity to be involved with several acquisitions and mergers. I witnessed very few situations where two companies merged together and ended up being better off. On paper, the mergers always look great. It is easy to make it appear attractive in black and white. In most cases, the lack of success has to do with management's failure to surface a new and greater *vision,* one that eclipses the individual visions of the competing companies.

Think of this same dynamic in the context of a typical marriage. A man and woman from different backgrounds often come together with opposing visions. Their failure to see a new and greater purpose for their lives as "one" can be a major force in the deterioration of a marriage. On the brink of a marital separation or divorce, you often hear the husband or wife admit, "Our lives were just heading in opposite directions," or "We just didn't have the same goals in life."

I have a theory about vision. I believe that the reason why most good teaching remains ineffective is because it lacks a context within which to be submitted. If there is not a context or encompassing vision, the information or teaching has less significance. The truth alone is not enough. One must know how to apply it and for what purpose.

The Power of Vision

Allow me to relate this idea to my own life. As a student, I struggled my way through school. Most of the teaching I received seemed to go in one ear and out the other. Feeling completely discouraged, I dropped out. Nothing seemed to register until I entered the business world and caught a *vision* and passion for my work. With a new and heightened sense of motivation, I returned to school and enrolled in day and evening courses that were centered around my newfound passion. The result was straight *A*s.

Let's look at another example. When Cindy and I were newlyweds, we set out to look for a new van that could tow our boat. It did not take long to find the perfect one. It was a bright orange Chevy van with mag wheels and chrome side pipes. It was the coolest thing

I had ever seen. We both wanted to buy it, but soon discovered that we were thirty dollars a month short of making the payments. At the time, that was considered quite a lot of money. Needless to say, Cindy and I went home disappointed that day.

At the same time that all of this was taking place, I was battling a bad habit. I was smoking four packs of cigarettes a day. I had made numerous attempts to quit with no success. Cigarettes at that time cost about twenty-five cents a pack. At that price, four packs a day amounted to thirty dollars a month, the exact amount we would need to buy that van.

So, I went to Cindy with a brilliant idea. I said, "Cindy, if I quit smoking we could afford that van." Of course she was thrilled with that idea and quickly agreed. My commitment had been made, and it was time to head off to the dealership. But before I was able to get one foot out the door, Cindy stopped me and suggested, "I think it would be best if you quit smoking *first*." I was so close! The issue was that I had behaved myself into a problem, and wisely enough, Cindy knew that I could not just talk myself out of it. There needed to be evidence of change.

Here is the bottom line for this true story. That night, I put down a four pack a day habit and never picked up another cigarette again. I wanted that van so badly—the *vision* was so strong—that I was able to chip away that nasty habit. This same power to overcome is available in every area of our lives, but only when coupled with true *vision*.

To this day, I find this principle powerfully at work. In my case it began with a van. Today it is an ongoing discovery of God's great purpose for my life, an unfolding of *His* vision. That is the ultimate motivation.

The Duel to Define

If you think about it, we pursue vision and purpose in life from two very opposing sources—the world and God. Some of us rely heavily on one over the other, and then there are those of us who turn to both. It is a spiritual duel and the winner will ultimately define who we are. Becoming aware of this battle was a major turning point for me, one that led to some serious introspection. I began to ask myself some tough questions. What or who am I allowing to define me? How much of what I am doing is being motivated by the world's vision for my life vs. God's vision?

I believe that each of us, every human being on the planet, is born with a spiritual vacancy that only God can fill. The world's attractions may satisfy us for the moment, but God's way of providing satisfaction is eternal. All that He asks of us is that we seek His will above our own. Until we truly understand what His will is, our lives will be marginal at best.

Confirming His Purpose

George Mueller, one of the most remarkable men of faith in the last two centuries, had a unique six-step plan to determine God's will:

> (1) I seek at the beginning to get my heart into such a state that it has no will of its own in regard to a given matter. (2) Having done this, I do not leave the result to feeling or simple impression. If I do so, I make myself vulnerable to great delusions. (3) I seek the will of the Spirit through, or in connection with, the Word of God. (4) Next, I take into account providential circumstances. These often plainly indicate God's will in connection with His will and Spirit. (5) I ask God in prayer to reveal His will to me aright. (6) Thus, through prayer to God, the study of the Word, and reflec-

> tion, I come to a deliberate judgment according to the best of my ability and knowledge.

More simply stated, there are *four factors* that need to line up before you can be sure you are sensing God's call or purpose in your life. They are as follows:

1. Read it in the Word
2. Hear it by His Spirit
3. Affirm it with wise, Godly counsel
4. See it in your circumstances

And never forget to precede each step with prayer!

Let's take a closer look at each step.

Read It in the Word

There are some people who believe that they can close their eyes, allow their Bible to flop open, point to a place on the page, and God will show them a verse that will guide them. I am not saying that God can't do that—He can do anything He likes. However, my experience suggests that this action borders more on superstition than on any common sense application of God's Word. When I suggest reading it in the Word, I am referring to seeing a pattern of God revealing something to you over significant time spent reading your Bible. Is there a message that is jumping off the pages?

Hear It by His Spirit

This is always the most difficult thing for me. I know that God speaks to us—my problem is that my mind is so active that it is hard for me to hear that still small voice. Someone once reminded me that wherever we go, there are thousands of radio waves in the air. Just because we can't see them does not minimize their existence. All we need is the right receiver to get tuned in. The same is true with hearing God. We must get tuned in to His voice.

Affirm It with Wise, Godly Counsel

Seek out your most mature Christian friends and loved ones. Find out if they agree with the direction that you are thinking of heading. My only caution here is to be discriminating and wise in choosing your counsel. I do believe that it takes a certain level of maturity in our relationship with God in order to discern whether something may be right for another person.

See It in Your Circumstances

Often life's circumstances provide a way for God to send us a signal of what He wants us to do. Is there something going on in your life which might indicate a new course or direction? Is there something that God is trying to get through to you?

I strongly suggest that you need all four of these areas to line up before pressing forward. I could tell you some tragic stories about people who impulsively reacted to two or three of these, only to discover they were headed down the wrong path.

An Unbelievable Experience

What I am about to share with you is the most incredible thing that has ever happened to me. It may even test and challenge some of your theology—it did mine. The event took place on 4 June 1994. I attended a meeting for the Rocky Mountain Christian Fellowship, a loosely associated group of pastors and leaders from the greater Denver area. This group came together once a month and typically brought in a guest speaker. I attended this meeting for the first time on the advice of a friend who thought it would be a great opportunity to network. Before telling you what took place that day, I want to set the stage by sharing some things that were going on in my life at that time.

Cindy and I were praying diligently about whether I should leave my executive position with Every Home for Christ (EHC) to launch a new ministry of my own. It was a challenging decision filled with much apprehension. Three out of the four things that I mentioned earlier were lined up solid. We were reading it in the Word—there was a pattern that both Cindy and I could not deny. We were also being affirmed through wise, Godly counsel—all of the people we looked up to and trusted both in Colorado and California were saying we should go for it. In addition, my position at EHC was no longer necessary. According to my circumstances, I was free to leave after five years of a successful turn-around management effort. We also experienced a significant equity increase in some real estate that would enable us to finance the new ministry start-up.

There was only one thing missing—we were not hearing God's voice. I wanted Him to scream at me. I can vividly remember the fear that we were battling at that time. Then it happened . . .

A Giant Fleece

After arriving at the Rocky Mountain Christian Fellowship meeting and greeting a few people, I sat down to enjoy the lunch that was being served. There were about eighty people in attendance. After our meal, they introduced the guest speaker—a man who they referred to as a prophet from Florida. By the way, I do not mean *prophet* in the natural gift sense. This man was someone who would hear from God and speak words of prophecy over people. Now I do not know what happens to you when someone is introduced as a prophet. As for me, I become very suspicious. I want to be clear in saying that my suspicion was not driven by a presupposition that God no longer speaks through people. I believe He does. It is just that I have witnessed too many situations where I found myself questioning the source.

During his thirty-minute talk, the speaker said that God had told him to come to this meeting and prophecy over pastors who had churches with less than seventy-five members. That seemed reasonable. Many pastors struggle when attendance is low. When he finished his talk he asked this small group of pastors to stand. There were eight in all. Some of them had their wives stand with them. Then he began to prophecy over them one at a time.

I had attended several of these types of meetings, but had never witnessed anything like this. The men were shaking and the women were weeping. This man was nailing things that he could never have known. His speech was not flowery. It was hard hitting. I was used to hearing things like, "God told me He wants to work on your marriage next month;" prophecy that was safe and predictably true. But this was different.

As the speaker continued to prophesy, I bowed my head and had a private chat with God. It went something like this, "God, it's me again. I know that You are getting tired of my fleeces and continual whining but, You know how scared I am. You know that I desire Your direction. Listen, Lord, I know that this man did not come here to prophecy to me, however, if You would use this man as Your vessel and speak to me through him—right now, in this very meeting—then I promise to listen and obey." It was a giant fleece!

I remember thinking as I was saying all of this—God sure must think I am dense. I could see Him looking down on me wondering when I would ever get it, when would I finally be able to hear Him? Well, after going through that dialogue, I looked up and realized that the speaker had run out of time. He apologized to the three pastors he did not have time to get to and proceeded to the podium where he entered into a closing prayer. All heads were bowed when in the middle of his prayer he suddenly stopped. The room was silent for an awkward amount of time. What was going on?

A few seconds later, I felt a hand on my shoulder. This man, someone I had never met, waded through a room of eighty people directly to me. Having seen my badge he said, "Vince, God just interrupted me and told me to come over here and give you a word." I was numb. He had me stand and follow him to the middle of the room. On the way over he asked me if I was a pastor. When I answered "No," he said, "That doesn't matter, God is stirring the gifts of *teaching* and *perceiving* in you," the two gifts that I score the highest on among the seven natural gifts. The mathematical odds of that alone are staggering. Then he went on to list every single fear that I had about starting my own ministry. He even mentioned that our children would join in our efforts. Shortly after this, through an absolute miracle, my oldest daughter Kim and her husband (an Air Force Academy graduate stationed in California), relocated back to Colorado Springs. Kim ran our ministry office for the first two years, and her younger sister Kristen has been with us ever since.

I get this picture of God up in heaven looking over this scene with outstretched arms and a big smile on His face saying, "Uh, D'Acchioli—anything else you need or will this finally do it for you?" I think He has great fun with us sometimes.

So why am I sharing this story with you? To somehow convey to you that I have an inside track on hearing God? Not at all! In fact, I wish that were true. I am sharing this because with all of my heart I believe that God will reveal His *vision* for us if we will just approach Him, be persistent and continue to seek Him.

The more I meet people who have ultimately discovered God's purpose for their lives, the more stories I hear, stories that are every bit as profound as the one you have just read.

I am convinced that in my case God knew that Cindy and I needed that fourth confirmation. He knew we would need that situation to look back on when the inevitable bouts with fear and doubt would come. He knew we needed to hear His voice. When I shared this experience with Cindy, we both knew what we had to do. The next week, I resigned from EHC, and the rest, as they say, is history.

Understanding the Four Forces

There are four forces at work in our lives every day: The *world*, the *flesh*, the *devil*, and the *Lord*. Understanding how these forces impact our lives is critical to discerning God's will. All four are competing for our attention all of the time.

First, there is the *world* and what it wants of you and me—trying to dictate how we should live our lives. Through movies, magazines, the workplace and other influencing experiences, we are being shaped and focused into a direction or course of action, sometimes without even knowing it. Not all of this is necessarily bad. It is only when we are following the world's direction at the expense of sensing God's. The world and all of its distractions can be a powerful negative force.

Second, there is our *flesh*. This has to do with our human nature. Our flesh wants what it wants and it wants it now. It is easy sometimes to follow the path of least resistance or go the way that seems like it might be more fun. An example of this might be that you have some godly friends giving you counsel to go in a direction that sounds good to you. You were already inclined to head that way, and after all, you just received wise and godly counsel. While it may be a tempting prospect, if the other three *factors* (mentioned earlier) are not present, it may not be God's will.

Third, there is the *devil.* If what I am saying about the importance of discovering *how* and *why* God made you is true, then guess who does not want you to discover it? The devil—that's right—the devil is real! He knows that when we finally discover our purpose in life his plans are thwarted. He will stop at nothing to send you off course. That is another reason why I feel it is so important to line up all four of the factors we previously discussed in order to realize God's will. God is not a God of disorder. There is very little chance that the enemy of our soul can find ways to deceive us if we sincerely and ardently seek to rely on God's wisdom rather than on our own.

Stepping Out Can Point the Way

Another way that we can help discover God's purpose for our lives is to exercise our natural gifts. As I mentioned at the end of the last chapter, sometimes as we step out and use the gifts God has given us, He reveals a new course or vision for our life. By now, you have surely identified at least some of your characteristics or strongest areas of giftedness. Now it's time to put that information to good use! As I mentioned earlier, if you have a *ministry* or *mercy* gift—volunteer for a mission trip or visit a hospital. If you are more inclined toward *administration* or *teaching*—take on a project or start a Bible study or small group.

In all of this, let me encourage you to also be patient. In Habakkuk 2:3 it says, "For the revelation awaits an appointed time; it speaks of the end and will not prove false. Though it linger, wait for it; it will certainly come and will not delay . . ."

Vision's Ultimate Promise

Michelangelo, the great painter and sculptor was once asked how he was able to create such masterful statues. His answer was something like, "I am not sure how it works exactly—but I am able to see the vision of the beautiful statue in the marble even before it is extracted from the rock quarry. You see, once I catch the vision, the rest is very simple—I just chip away what does not belong."

That is the great promise of God's wonderful vision for us. Once we catch it, we are never the same. I have witnessed it in my own life and in the lives of countless others. Don't give up. Pursue God and His plan for your life. Use your gifts first and foremost to glorify Him and you will soon discover an unmatched sense of personal fulfillment!

"Being confident of this, that He who began a good work in you will carry it on to completion until the day of Christ Jesus." (Phil. 1:6)

Chapter Summary

1. Vision is a powerful force that can set the context for our life.
2. There are two sources dueling to define who we are—the world—and God.
3. Before acting on what you believe to be God's call or purpose for your life, refer to the *Four Factors*:
    1) Read it in the word.
    2) Hear it by His Spirit.
    3) Affirm it with wise, godly counsel.
    4) See it in your circumstances.
4. Sometimes in the exercising of your natural gifts God reveals His purpose or vision for your life.

Discussion Questions:

1. What are some examples of the world's definition of meaning and purpose vs. God's?
2. Who or what is winning the battle in defining who you are today?
3. What are some practical ways that you can exercise your gifts right now?

Write down one or two key ideas that you gleaned from this chapter and at least one new behavior you would like to start practicing.

Key Ideas

____

____

____

____

New Behavior/Commitment

____

____

____

____

Coming Up in Chapters 5 & 6:

In the next two chapters we will discover why grasping hold of God's plan for our lives is so important. He chooses to use you and me to advance His kingdom here on earth. What an awesome privilege that is.

Chapter Five

Understanding Our Challenge

"As fish are caught in a cruel net, or birds are taken in a snare, so men are trapped by evil times that fall unexpectedly upon them" (Eccl. 9:12).

Now that you have realized that there is a divine purpose for your life, let's discuss how you have been *wired* to *work*. I chose the phrase, "wired to work" as the title of this book because it holds two life-affirming implications. First, you have been uniquely equipped, or *wired* with the appropriate gifts to fulfill your God-given purpose. Second, you have been called for a purpose, to go *to work*. Whether we choose to acknowledge it or not, as Christians, we have a lifelong assignment. There is work to be done toward the advancement of God's kingdom. Allow me to set the stage for our challenge.

The State of Our Nation

The 2000 presidential election and the incredible aftermath have provided us with some powerful insights into our nation's condition—if we are willing to see them. At no time in our history have we been so divided and mean spirited. In my view, our reaction to circumstances as a people is much more important than who we ultimately elect to lead us.

So what has brought us to this point? Ever since the fall of man in the garden, the human race has been separated from its Creator. This separation, just like a child's separation from a parent, causes insecurity. Mankind has been looking for security ever since we put on those first fig leaves. The absence of security usually brings on fear and anger. Where God is present in a relationship, this can be overcome, resulting in peace and joy.

This same illustration can be applied on a national level. We have taken God out of almost every aspect of our national life. If it is true that there is no *real* security apart from Him, then what is the logical result? In our unquenchable desire to find this security we ultimately form gangs. I am not just talking about the violent and often criminal gangs that roam many of our city streets. The same mentality that produced these gangs has also separated us as a people into countless groups—or herds—that have the same effect. It's the "my-way-is the-right-way" attitude.

Let me list just a few of these gangs for you:

Democrats, Republicans, right, left, liberal, moderate, conservative, big business, pro-life, pro-choice, environmentalists, Protestant, Catholic, Jewish, Muslim, Mormon, Evangelical, Charismatic, Pentecostal, gay, lesbian, black, brown, red, yellow and the list goes on . . .

Why do kids join gangs? For acceptance, a sense of family, being a part of something bigger than themselves—the ability to advance their own views—security. Because many young people are not getting a sense of security from their own families and refuse to turn to God, they ultimately gravitate toward an environment that makes them feel safe or a part of something special. Is this a counterfeit for the real thing? Yes, but it seems to satisfy the needs they feel.

I want to suggest to you that most adults join gangs for many of the same reasons. Even if our initial affiliation is honest and with worthy intent, there is the potential for our involvement to escalate to a need to feel good about ourselves. When this happens, our own needs will often trump the worthiness of our causes.

God's original plan was for man to find security in relationship with Him and within the natural family structure. As these relationships break down, they leave behind a vacuum of insecurity that begs to be filled. Where do I go? As recently as twenty years ago, the job environment was a temporary, though counterfeit, place to find some sense of security. Today, however, that is no longer the case. The thought of lifetime job security is now a myth. It is no wonder that we gravitate toward other sources in order to fill one of our greatest needs.

Fueling the Fire

Enter modern media. Today's media have become big business. Big business is about generating money, and in the media, money is generated by ratings. And what receives higher ratings than controversy?

Now, let's return to the aftermath of our recent election. Can you remember even one news broadcast that generated a balanced and sensible view or solution? Rather, what you observed were two or more people representing their own gang's point of view, sometimes in the most animated and mean-spirited ways imaginable. After all, "My group's position is the only right one to consider. We have the moral high ground," they would spew. The media thrive on this kind of political banter, and, sadly, so do we. The result is what we find in our culture today, a highly flammable level of polarization. The only difference between street gangs and those listed above is that most of the latter are not carrying guns and knives—yet!

Eugenia Price, in her 1966 book, *The Wider Place*, wrote:

> Sooner or later most of us reach the point in our lives where we must choose either to follow blindly the patterns of our conditioning, conforming to our special groups' emphasis so as not to be an outsider, or to enter alone with God, if necessary, the wider place where we dare to permit God to set the standards. If we choose at this critical point in our lives, to follow the herd merely for protection and acceptance, we begin the respectable, sure road to bondage.

Who Should We Blame?

During one of my speaking engagements, I asked for a show of hands from those who felt that we were headed in the right direction as a nation. I was not surprised by the lack of response. Those who truly know God and understand His precepts would likely find it difficult to be encouraged about where our society is heading. I then asked my audience another question, "Where would you place the blame for our current condition?"

An easy and somewhat popular answer to this question might be, "It's the fault of our political leaders who have failed us, the government, or Hollywood and the movie industry." While it is true that these are all powerful influences, we cannot hold them solely responsible. Apart from God, man will always have a tendency to follow the way of the world. Now don't miss this. I am about to make an incredibly bold proclamation: The blame for the condition of today's society belongs squarely at the foot of the church of Jesus Christ. If we, as a body of believers, do not accept the responsibility for our condition, we are ignoring the mandate that God has given us.

Why? It is and always has been God's plan for the world to be transformed by His love through those of us who truly know Him. In fact, I have often said that God's plan for planet earth is very simple. It can be distilled into one sentence:

An invisible God is made visible through the actions of those who fellowship with His Son Jesus.

I don't know why God chose you and me to impact our world—but He did. His ultimate intention is for us to be transformed into the likeness of Jesus.

"For those God foreknew He also predestined to be conformed to the likeness of his Son" (Rom. 8:29).

The evolution of a form-over-substance culture and mentality has crept into the church of Jesus Christ. For the first time in our history, our culture is having a more significant impact upon the church than the church is having on the culture. Sadly, we live in a country that has developed a form of Christianity that is a mile wide and half an inch deep. We have a lot of Christ-sounding people, but very few that are genuinely Christ-like. As a result, our culture views us more as a political movement than a spiritual one. Frankly, we deserve the label. There are plenty of Christians yelling "baby killer" from picket lines near abortion clinics, but where are they when that 14-year-old little girl is on the front steps of the clinic at 4:30 in the afternoon—sobbing uncontrollably?

This can't be the kind of Christianity that Jesus envisioned. I believe that Jesus would be sitting right next to that little girl, not agreeing with what she did any more than He agreed with the sin of the woman at the well. I can imagine Him sitting there with His arm around her, telling her how much He loved her and encouraging her to follow Him. I wonder how many future abortions could be prevented in the life of this 14-year-old if someone were there for her with the life and love of Jesus. Perhaps you would have chosen the same Christ-like approach. If so, I encourage you to stay on course. But realize that you are in the minority.

The Way We Look

Let me give you some hard-hitting examples that illustrate how many nonbelievers view Christians. I want you to imagine that I am standing next to a radical feminist and I say to her, "Tell me, what is the first thing that comes to your mind when I say the words *evangelical Christian man?"* I do not know exactly how she would respond, but I am somewhat confident that you would not hear, "Boy, you talk about a man who knows how to love a woman, someone who knows how precious a woman is and how to serve her—that is the kind of man every woman is looking for."

What if we were to ask the same question to a man caught up in the homosexual lifestyle, "Tell me, sir, what comes to your mind when I say *evangelical Christian*?" The response may vary slightly from person to person, but it is not likely that you would hear, "Wow, those people are really something. They do not approve of my lifestyle—they say it is sinful—but I'll tell you what—I've never felt such love and compassion from a group of people in my whole life. They are out there building and running hospices—their love and care is unconditional." As a Christian, do you ever wonder where Jesus would be hanging out if He were living here among us today?

Here is a third example for good measure. Suppose we asked the same question to a board member for the National Education Association, "Tell me, what is the first thing that comes to your mind when I say *evangelical Christian*?" Answers may vary, but I doubt you would hear, "Those are the kids we want in our schools—the parents we want on our boards—they work hard and want to help bring about a better system—they are extremely encouraging and caring." Now I want to make another bold statement, *we will never turn our country around as long as the current perception of Christianity prevails.*

Realistically, we will never be able to change everyone's heart. There will always be those who will do or say whatever is needed to support their personal cause. The masses, however, have bought into this stereotype primarily because the media continue to portray us in a very negative light. We are not giving them a strong enough counter. Too many of us talk-the-talk and fall short on walking-the-walk. I call it "sound-bite Christianity."

If you find yourself struggling with my theory, let me give you one more thing to think about. Hypothetically, imagine for a moment that the three individuals we just confronted have never met or known a true evangelical Christian. Instead, they have literally walked and talked with Jesus Himself—in His physical person. What if I were to repeat the same questions again, only this time I asked, "What is the first thing that comes to your mind when I say *Jesus*?" Do you think that their response would be any different? Well of course Vince, but that's not fair—after all, that's *Jesus*. That's right, and what is God's plan? That this same Jesus is seen in you and me.

Perhaps this powerful illustration will help. Have you ever seen the famous painting of the Mona Lisa? If you have not had the privilege of viewing the original painting, perhaps you have seen a photograph or print. Can you recall what the frame looked like? Probably not. If that frame had flashing Christmas lights on it you might remember. Why? Because it would draw attention to itself. You see the job of a good frame is not to draw attention to itself, but rather to complement or highlight the picture. In much the same way, you and I ought to be like that frame. If people are seeing too much of us, and not enough of Jesus (through us), then we are failing our purpose.

The world around us is hurting and lost. People are desperately looking for the *real deal.* Who is going to give that to them if not the followers of Christ?

How Did We Get Here?

While speaking to a group of local pastors recently, I asked the following question, "Pastor, what is your *product*?" I could tell that some of them were a little intimidated by my use of business terminology. I explained that my question was not meant to address them personally, but rather the broader aspect of the Church. In other words, if the Church were a factory, what should its product be?

Many of these men had a difficult time articulating a response. Finally, after a few minutes had passed, I initiated a second question, "What is Chrysler's product?" The immediate response was "cars." I then suggested that while it is true that they do assemble cars, cars are not really their product. As confusion began to break out, I continued, "Chrysler's product is really transportation. They manufacture different kinds of cars to satisfy a wide range of transportation needs."

The pastors seemed to readily accept this notion. I then restated my first question, "So, using this illustration, what is *your* product?" One gentleman readily answered, "The product of the local Church is to produce *Christ-like people.*" What a great response! We should be producing people who truly reflect Jesus. However, aren't *Christ-like people* really like cars? You see I believe that the product of the Church ought to be *a godly world.* It would follow, then, that the product of a church in Colorado Springs ought to be a godly Colorado Springs. I wanted these pastors to see the big picture. Just as Chrysler remembers each time they manufacture a car that their purpose is to satisfy and provide transportation needs, we as the Church need to recognize that the purpose of building up *Christ-like people* is to produce godliness in a hurting world.

I continued my teaching that day with a challenging question, "Most of us would agree that Chrysler is doing a pretty good job in delivering a quality product, now tell me, how do you think the church is doing?" After a brief time of reflection, I followed with this final illustration:

Let's assume that Chrysler has gone out and purchased the best raw materials available. At this point, they throw all of this rubber, glass, metal, plastic, etc. into a box on the factory floor and call it a car. Clearly, we would never identify this box of parts as a car. It could never lead to transportation. Now I want you to think of an average man or woman sitting in church receiving the greatest raw material the world has ever known (not since Jesus walked the planet, have we been equipped with such extraordinary wisdom and knowledge). To think that this man or woman will step out of that building a *Christ-like person* is as ludicrous as believing that a box of parts is a car.

So, how should we go about solving this problem? Chrysler figured out a system that we, as the Body of Christ, should consider and employ. First, they went to the drawing board and asked themselves an important question, *"What is this car supposed to look like?"* Then they drew up every detail. With a clear *vision* in mind, they initiated an assembly line. They realized that they could not attach the wheel before the axle or the engine before the frame. (It's interesting that in the academic community, we know that you do not teach advanced calculus to a first grader, yet somehow we have lost that concept when trying to develop *Christ-like people.*) For Chrysler, the work is done part-upon-part, for us it should be done in a similar manner, precept-upon-precept.

In continuing their process, Chrysler does not stop at the assembly line. They do not want to take any chances. Before one of their cars is allowed to leave the factory, they send a person with a clipboard down to the end of the line. This person is required to give the car a thorough inspection. Then they go to the check box on top of the form that asks, "Is this product ready to represent our company?" If the answer is yes, a check goes in the box and the car is out the door.

Intentional Christianity

Could it be that our lack of spiritual depth stems from the fact that we have failed to apply this same kind of process in training the followers of Christ? The church must begin to practice what I have coined *Intentional Christianity*, or Christianity with a purpose.

In the business world, when sales are down, management calls a time out. They want to pinpoint their problem and make a deliberate attempt to find a solution. The time has come for the Body of Christ to call a collective time-out. We need to rediscover our *vision.* It's time to rise to the occasion and walk as God intended. Now is the time to rethink our strategy, to change our mindset, to change our world!

The Evolution of Our Culture

Years ago, I developed a chart (refer to page 98) to illustrate the direction of our future as a nation. My premise is that there are only two ways to govern man: God's way and man's way. God's way of governing is an inside-out process. The heart is changed first, making it possible for the basic laws governing man to be effective.

If we choose to ignore God's influence on our culture, there is only one other way to govern—man's way. The humanistic way of creating social order is an outside-in process. Rules and regulations take the form of law in an effort to shape and mold behavior. I would estimate that we have more legislation in the United States than in any other country in the history of the world. Laws are a crucial and necessary part of our coexistence. However, it should be obvious that law, in-and-of-itself, is not the answer.

In studying the chart on the following page, you will notice the sharp contrast between God's way of governing and man's way. Make no mistake about it, we are cruising down the right side of the chart at amazing speed.

Rather than taking the time to elaborate on the depth of this crisis, I would like to direct your attention to a few researchers who have already done an outstanding job at this task. For example, Chuck Colson has written extensively about our current condition. I highly recommend his work. George Barna, a noted Christian researcher, has spent years surveying the landscape and has produced reports, some of which will astound you. After asking questions on most social issues, he contends that there is a blur between Christians and nonbelievers. I encourage you to discover these sources and browse through some of their findings.

What Are We Missing?

Some time ago I had the privilege of speaking in one of our country's largest African-American churches. I want to share my experience with you in an attempt to convey my belief regarding what we must do to change our circumstances.

That Sunday morning, I brought a teaching on intimacy with God. In the midst of my sermon, rather

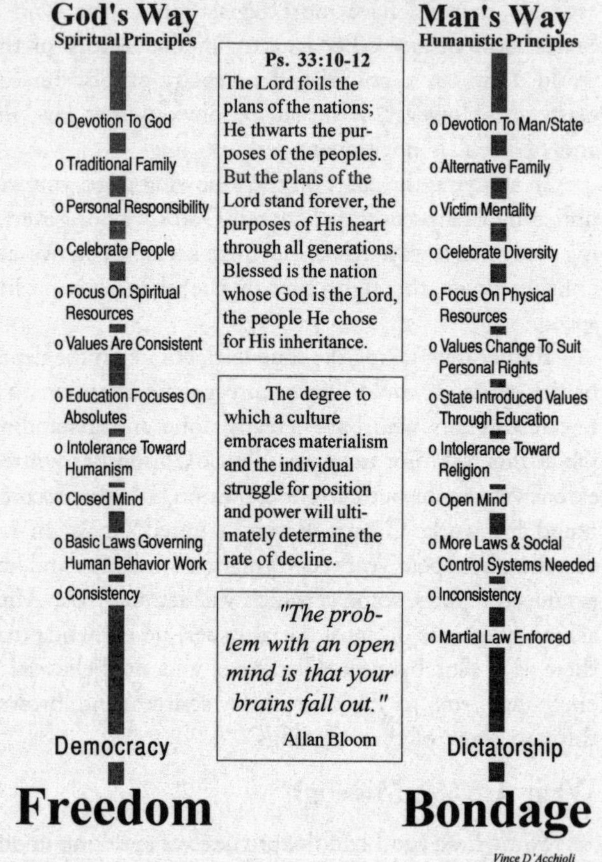

spontaneously, I shouted out, "I am sick and tired of racial reconciliation." Talk about controversial! I quickly followed that statement up with an appeal for my audience to hear me out, to hear my heart. I continued, "We have more laws on the books in the US today to encourage racial reconciliation then in any other nation in the history of the world. I am not suggesting that these laws are unnecessary. We need them to maintain some sense of social order. But the question remains, are these laws solving the problem?"

I continued, "What about talk? There is more talk about racial reconciliation today than ever before. Promise Keepers is making a valiant effort to lead the way with a clarion call to *break down the walls*. This kind of discussion is important, and should not be minimized as an influential tactic. But is talking about it getting the job done?" Most people in my audience gestured "no."

I went on to explain, "The way I see it, we have two choices: We could quit trying and accept the notion that racial reconciliation will never be possible or we could recognize that maybe we haven't found the right formula to solve the problem. Maybe we are missing something." Obviously, the first possibility is not an option. The Bible is very clear that we are to be reconciled as a people. The Lord would never have instructed us in this way if it were not feasible. Therefore, we are left with the second choice. We have yet to find the winning formula. What could it be?

As our service drew to a close, I asked my audience (and I ask you), "Think about someone you know. I don't care what color his or her skin is, where he or she is from or what he or she has done. Think of a person you know who is radically in love with Jesus, a person who has Jesus' blood pumping through his or her veins, a role model of what it is like to be truly intimate with God. Can you think of anyone who fits that description who has a racist bone in his or her body?" I concluded my message that morning with something to dwell on, "Perhaps these people have found the missing formula that we have all been looking for."

Reconciliation Begins at the Cross

What is the missing formula that will inevitably lead us to spiritual maturity and reconciliation? *Reconcile yourself to Jesus!* Why? Because until we are able to see others through the Lord's eyes, there is no way that we can truly love or appreciate the differences among us. His view sees beyond the surface, deep into the heart and soul of a person, and His love is unconditional.

Let's quit placing blame. Instead of focusing our attention on each other, let's begin to focus on getting closer to Jesus. Everything else will take care of itself. No amount of political maneuvering, law making or rhetoric will ever substitute for the power of Jesus and His unparalleled love. Position Him at the center of your decisions and relationships and begin to witness the incredible results! Love the Lord your God . . . and then, and only then, will you truly be able to love your neighbor.

Hope Lies in Our Response

I want to conclude this chapter with one final illustration, one that I pray will offer a bit of hope to this situation. If you have ever read the book of Ecclesiastes, you know that it contains the musings of a man who was commonly referred to as the wisest man in history. His name was Solomon. Throughout Ecclesiastes, Solomon did what many of us would call a lot of whining about life. In fact, there are well over fifty occasions where Solomon is found complaining. "Chasing after wind" is repeated nine times; "all is vanity" is quoted thirty-three times; the word "meaningless" is used thirty-five times.

But what I find most interesting is Solomon's final discourse. It is found in Ecclesiastes 12:13, "Now all has been heard; here is the conclusion of the matter: Fear God and keep His commandments, for this is the whole duty of man. For God will bring every deed into judgment, including every hidden thing, whether it is good or evil."

The message is clear. In the light of despair we need to *fear God* and *keep His commandments.* (In the context above, *fear* is translated as respect or being in awe of God.) So what is the bottom line for us? Revere God and keep (or *do*) His commandments. There is hope, and it lies in our response!

Chapter Summary:

1. The cultural influence upon the church is greater than the church's influence upon the culture.
2. God's plan is simple—that an invisible God is made visible through the actions of those who fellowship with His Son, Jesus.
3. What is missing in the Body of Christ is true *Christ-likeness.*
4. Our only hope is to *fear* (revere) God and keep (obey) His commandments.

Discussion Questions:

1. Can you list some examples of things you have experienced or seen that may indicate that we are going in the wrong direction as a nation?
2. What has this discussion meant to you personally? Has it opened your eyes to anything new? If so, what?

Write down one or two key ideas that you gleaned from this chapter and at least one new behavior you would like to start practicing.

Key Ideas

____

____

____

____

New Behavior/Commitment

____

____

____

____

Coming Up in Chapter Six:

Let's create a plan of action. Chapter six will explain, in detail, what we must *do* to make a difference in our world. This is a key discussion. Now that you have a better understanding of *how* and *why* God made you, it is time to *go to work*.

Chapter Six

Making a Difference: Real Christianity in an Unreal World

It is clear to me that our loving response to the people and situations around us is the key to truly *making a difference*. The world is looking for the *real deal* and where are they going to see it, if not from fully devoted followers of Jesus? In this chapter I want to explore what we must *do* to have a lasting impact upon others. We have talked about *how* and *why* God made us, now let's discuss our call. What are we to *do* with what God has given us?

Our Call

Jesus, while on the Mount of Olives said, "It's like a man going away: He leaves his house and puts his servants in charge, each with his assigned task, and tells the one at the door to keep watch. Therefore keep watch because you do not know when the owner of the house will come back—whether in the evening, or at midnight, or when the rooster crows, or at dawn. If he comes suddenly, do not let him find you sleeping. What I say to you, I say to everyone: Watch!" (Mark 13:34-37).

This verse is suggesting two things: First, we must be aware, *watch* what is going on around us. We are called to be watchmen. (I hope that this book has in some way helped you in this area.) Second, we are called to *work*. Jesus says that we each have an assigned task. I trust that you are now a little closer to understanding your task or purpose.

Now lets look at the Apostle Paul's last words to Timothy,

> In the presence of God and of Christ Jesus, who will judge the living and the dead, and in view of His appearing and His kingdom, I give you this charge: Preach the Word; be prepared in season and out of season; correct, rebuke and encourage with great patience and careful instruction. For the time will come when men will not put up with sound doctrine. Instead, to suit their own desires, they will gather around them a great number of teachers to say what their itching ears want to hear. They will turn their ears away from the truth and turn aside to myths. But you (that means you and me), keep your head in all situations, endure hardship, do the work of an evangelist, discharge all the duties of your ministry. (2 Tim. 4:1-5)

After describing a time to come, (which accurately characterizes where we are today), Paul calls Timothy and all of us to discharge all the duties of our ministry. This is a command that is not to be taken lightly. However, the problem for many is not in understanding the command, but rather in understanding *how* to carry it out.

What to *Do*

In the following verses, I have italicized some operative words that I would like you to notice.

Galatians 6:7-10: "Do not be deceived: God cannot be mocked. A man reaps what he sows. The one who sows to please his sinful nature, from that nature will reap destruction; the one who sows to please the Spirit, from the Spirit will reap eternal life."

"Let us not become weary in *doing* good, for at the proper time we will reap a harvest if we do not give up. Therefore, as we have opportunity, let us *do* good to all people, especially to those who belong to the family of believers" (emphasis added).

Titus 2:11-14: "For the grace of God that brings salvation has appeared to all men. It teaches us to say 'No' to ungodliness and worldly passions, and to live self-controlled, upright and godly lives in this present age, while we wait for the blessed hope—the glorious appearing of our great God and Savior, Jesus Christ, who gave Himself for us to redeem us from all wickedness and to purify for Himself a people that are His very own, eager to *do* what is good" (emphasis added).

Ephesians 2:10: "For we are God's workmanship, created in Christ Jesus to *do* good works, which God prepared in advance for us *to do*" (emphasis added).

Philippians 2:3-4: "*Do* nothing out of selfish ambition or vain conceit, but in humility consider others better than yourselves. Each of you should look not only to your own interests, but also to the interests of others" (emphasis added).

John 4:31-34: "Meanwhile His disciples urged Him, 'Rabbi, eat something.' But he said to them, 'I have food to eat that you know nothing about.' Then His disciples said to each other, 'Could someone have brought Him food?' 'My food,' said Jesus, 'is to *do* the will of Him who sent me and to finish His work' " (emphasis added).

Proverbs 21:3: "To *do* what is right and just is more acceptable to the Lord than sacrifice" (emphasis added).

These verses give us a powerful picture of the importance of *doing* rather than *talking*. The idea here is that it is important how we live and love, and not just what we say or our clever Christian arguments.

Four Principles That Will Make a Difference

It is time to form a new paradigm. I want to share with you four principles that I believe we must have in order to impact our world. My prayer is that they will help you put into practice many of the ideas you have learned in this book.

1. *Adopt Behavior That Lights Up*

> You are the light of the world. A city on a hill cannot be hidden. Neither do people light a lamp and put it under a bowl. Instead they put it on its stand, and it gives light to everyone in the house. In the same way, *let* your light shine before men, that they may see your good deeds and praise your Father in heaven. (Matt. 5:14-16, emphasis added)

Do we *let* our light shine, or are we shining it? Sometimes when we shine our light, all others see is the glare. I remember Pastor Jack Hayford standing on the platform one Sunday, holding a tiny birthday candle. He asked for all the lights in the sanctuary to be turned out. At that point, there was only enough light from that candle to see just a few feet around him. But, those of us in the remotest part of the room could still see him. That very small amount of light was able to illuminate his countenance, even from a great distance.

It was a powerful illustration of how we are to live our lives. Not as people who have some corner on the truth and are shining a condemning light on the sins of others, but rather, as people content to live a life that lights up. Philippians 2:15 says, "So that you may become blameless and pure, children of God without fault in a crooked and depraved generation, in which you *shine* like stars in the universe."

Now look at what 1 Peter 2:12 has to say, "Keep your *behavior* excellent among the Gentiles, so that in the thing in which they slander you as evildoers, they may on account of your good deeds, as they observe them, glorify God in the day of visitation" (emphasis added).

I also like what Paul states in the Living Bible translation of 2 Corinthians,

> Are we beginning to be like those false teachers of yours who must tell you all about themselves and bring long letters of recommendation with them? I think you hardly need someone's letter to tell you about us, do you? And we don't need a recommendation from you either. The only letter I need is you yourselves! By looking at the good change in your hearts, everyone can see that we have done a good work among you. *They can see that you are a letter from Christ*, written by us. It is not a letter written with pen and ink, but by the Spirit of the living God; not one carved on stone, but in human hearts. (2 Cor. 3:1-3, emphasis added)

We need to be *letters from Christ.* I love that line. Isn't that what you want to be? My friend, none of this is possible unless we are willing and able to live *Christlike* lives. Saint Francis once said, "Go out and witness to people, and if necessary, use words." People need to *see* Jesus, not just hear about Him.

Are You a Stranger?

First Peter 2:11-12 says, "Dear friends, I urge you, as aliens and *strangers* in the world, to abstain from sinful desires, which war against your soul. Live such good lives among the pagans that, though they accuse you of doing wrong, they may see your good deeds and glorify God on the day He visits us."

The Bible is filled with passages encouraging us to be different, separate, and strangers in this world. This is very often a challenge, particularly if you are what I call a politically motivated Christian. By that I mean someone who believes that the truth of Christ is something that can be communicated to people who do not believe and somehow they ought to just lay hold of it. Perhaps that was applicable fifty years ago, but certainly not today. People need to *see* it lived out before they will believe it.

We must also remember that the Bible calls us citizens of a heavenly kingdom. Yet, at the same time, we are also citizens here in a free country. Those are two very different privileges and suggest two very different approaches. As citizens of a free country, you and I have the right of speaking out through our votes. As citizens of a heavenly kingdom, our job is to communicate a message with our lives.

Sadly, we often want people to respond to our complaints rather than our lives. Our divorce rate is the same as the rest of the world, yet we espouse *family values*. Why should anyone buy into our version of the truth?

How Do I Look?

I had an experience a few years ago that exemplifies how the world sometimes views us as Christians.

The occasion was a chapel service I was asked to speak at for a ministry in Colorado Springs, Colorado. There were about one hundred people there, mostly evangelical Christians from different church backgrounds. Before I began my talk I planted someone in the audience that I wanted to call on later. I told him that at some point I was going to look at him and I wanted him to ask me a question that I had given him. Unsure of my intent, he agreed to follow my instruction.

That day, I introduced myself as a Christian man named Bob. I went on to explain, "I attend a large Christian church here in town and I love the Lord. Jesus is really neat and the Bible is a great book. Of course it's not really relevant anymore today." Immediately some of my spectators began to look at each other as if to say, "Did I hear what I thought I heard?"

Still in character, I continued, "It is so wonderful to have so many different religions, isn't it? After all they help so many of us arrive at our true potential, our real karma." That did it. Now I could see some real tensions beginning to rise. By the way, the person I am describing is often called a *cultural Christian*. There are more people who believe this way than you may think.

I concluded with a question, "What do you *do* with a guy like that?" Please notice my choice of words. I did not say, "What do you *say* to a guy like that?" One by one they began to raise their hands. I vividly remember the first response, "Bob, you call yourself a Christian?" "Yes, I do." "Well, do you believe that Jesus was the Son of God, and in fact was God?" "Why no, where did you get a ridiculous notion like that?"

It was like a lightning bolt went through my audience. My crowd was on the edge of their seats and hands were flying up all over the room. The same man continued, "It's right here in the Bible." I interrupted, "I already told you about the Bible. It's a great book, but it's not relevant. How can you believe that nonsense?"

Things were getting tense. The audience started to challenge me about my belief that all religions were good and I confounded them with examples out of the Bible that they could not speak to. Unfortunately many people who try to use the Bible to argue their point don't know enough about it to really cement their case. I let it get to a feverish pitch, until the faces that stared back at me were filled with disgust. They hoped for someone, anyone to be able to corner me—to really zing me good.

Then I turned to my plant in the audience. He raised his hand and I acknowledged his question. "Bob, would you consider coming over to my house for dinner on Friday night?" Sure, I said, I would be delighted. The room went deafeningly quiet. People were bewildered. What was that? What did that have to do with our interaction? I then explained, "What you just witnessed is the key to our response as Christians. I am going to go over to this man's house on Friday night. While there, I will have an opportunity to *see* how he conducts his life, how he treats his wife and kids. This experience alone will do more for the cause of Christ in my life than any argument that has just been spoken in this room." Occasionally, we must take a look in the mirror and realize how we are coming across to those who do not share our beliefs.

Watch This

Allow me to carry this principle further with a more personal illustration. While teaching in the business world, I once led a meeting on how to train employees. In an effort to make a particular point, I found a willing participant in my audience that was a smoker. I asked him if he would teach me how to smoke. I had never done it and I needed help. He agreed and handed me a cigarette. He then said that the first thing I should do is put it in my mouth. So, I took the cigarette and put the whole thing inside my mouth. Then in absolute disgust I spit it out and complained, "That is awful! If that was smoking, I don't want any part of it!"

My fellow instructor was dumbfounded and responded, "That was not smoking." He quickly handed me another cigarette and asked me to just listen this time around. "You see this white part? That is the tobacco. The brown part on the end is the filter. I want you to put only the filter end in your mouth." So I broke off the brown end and popped it into my mouth. I thought his eyes were going to come out of his head. The audience broke into laughter. I reiterated, "This still does not seem right." We proceeded to go through almost a whole pack of cigarettes, all of which ended up in a heap on the floor. Then it happened. A young man, obviously frustrated, came steaming down the aisle, grabbed the cigarettes and lighter from my volunteer and said, "STOP! WATCH ME!" What a powerful example of how important it is for people to *see* something lived out before grasping a hold of it themselves.

I recently came across this great poem by Edgar A. Guest:

> I'd rather see a sermon than hear one any day
>
> I'd rather one should walk with me
than merely show the way
>
> The eye's a better pupil and more willing than the ear
>
> Fine counsel is confusing, but example's always clear
>
> The best of all the preachers are
the men who live their creeds
>
> For, to see the good in action is what everybody needs
>
> I can soon learn how to do it if you'll let me see it done
>
> I can watch your hand in action
though your tongue too fast may run
>
> All the lectures you deliver may be very wise and true
>
> But I'd rather learn my lesson by observing what you do
>
> For I may misunderstand you and
the fine advice you give
>
> But there's no misunderstanding how you
act and how you live

In closing out this first principle, let me ask you, are you imposing or exposing your faith? Are you shining your light or letting it shine? Are you planting seeds or pulling weeds? It is time to stop cursing the darkness and become a candle.

In John 12:47 Jesus says, "For I did not come to judge the world, but to save it." Jesus did not say I did not come to judge but I am sending you to do that. Yet, that is how many see their role. The Bible goes on to say in John 16:8, "When He comes, He will convict the world of guilt in regard to sin and righteousness and judgment." Christian, it is not your job.

It would be good for us to heed the words of Colossians 4:5-6, "Be wise in the way you *act* toward outsiders; make the most of every opportunity. Let your conversation be always full of grace, seasoned with salt, so that you may know how to answer everyone."

2. Develop a Healthy Attitude Toward Others

In psychology, there exists a theory called the Pygmalion Effect. The Pygmalion Effect suggests that our attitude and assumptions about people can actually contribute to their being that way. Imagine that I just hired someone to work for me and during the first week I observe something in him that causes me to conclude that he is under qualified. I think to myself, he will never make it here. The Pygmalion Effect says that I will unconsciously behave in ways that will bring about his departure, like a self-fulfilling prophecy.

I heard about a study that was done back in the fifties to test this theory. Behavioral scientists took an eighth grade class with twenty students and assigned them a teacher. In doing so, they also identified five particular students as gifted, and communicated this knowledge to their instructor. At the end of the year the scientists tested each student to determine how much they had learned. The five gifted students were off the charts. They had learned fifteen to thirty percent more than the rest of the class.

Later, they broke the news to the teacher. They had never even tested the so-called "gifted students" before sending them into her classroom. Rather, they randomly selected five boys and girls and suggested that they were gifted. In light of this experiment, I wonder how our education system would be affected if our teachers truly believed that every child in their class was gifted.

Proverbs 16:3 encourages us to commit our *works* to the Lord, and then our *thoughts* will be established. What does this mean? The operative words here are *works,* or what we do, and *thoughts,* how we think. If we behave in the right way then our thinking can be impacted. In other words, attitude follows behavior. Jesus would not have said "Love your enemy," if you were never going to have any. If you don't know of any now, chances are, you will at some point. Your attitude and subsequent response to them is the key.

Luke 6:27-28 says, "But I tell you who hear me: Love your enemies, do good to those who hate you, bless those who curse you, pray for those who mistreat you."

No one was better at poking fun and telling off-color jokes about our political leaders than me. I was a champion, that is until the Lord convicted me. What right do I, or any of us for that matter, have to poke fun at or demean others? You have read my testimony and know that my life was not exemplary. And yet here you are reading my book. We cannot give up on anyone! When Paul wrote that we should be praying for those in authority over us, Nero was in command. Today's leaders cannot be compared to the wickedness of this man.

I remember a pastor saying once that if you are not praying for those whom you do not like or agree with, you are leaving a spiritual vacuum that something is going to get sucked into. Is that what we want? The bottom line is that you cannot love someone if your attitude toward him or her is not right. We need to be gracious and give people the benefit of the doubt. Where would you and I be if our wonderful Lord had not done that with us?

3. Be Diligent and Get Out of Your Comfort Zone

Look at what happens in Numbers 32:1-7:

> The Reubenites and Gadites, who had very large herds and flocks, saw that the lands of Jazer and Gilead were suitable for livestock. So they came to Moses and Eleazar the priest and to the leaders of the community, and said, "Ataroth, Dibon, Jazer, Nimrah, Heshbon, Elealeh, Sebam, Nebo and Beon. The land the Lord subdued before the people of Israel are suitable for livestock, and your servants have livestock. If we have found favor in your eyes," they said, "let this land be given to your servants as our possession. Do not make us cross the Jordan." Moses said to the Gadites and Reubenites, "Shall your countrymen go to war while you sit here? Why do you discourage the Israelites from going over into the land the Lord has given them?"

At times, we are just like the Gadites and Reubenites. We get comfortable where we are and don't want to jump in. Or perhaps we buy into the lie that says, "What can I do? After all, I am just one person. How can I possibly make a difference?"

Do you remember the Bible story about the little boy feeding the five thousand with just a few loaves and fishes? Let me offer you a little different version of how that scene could have gone:

> Jesus.
>
> Yes, little boy.
>
> There are a lot of people here and it is just about time to eat—what should we do?
>
> Well, what do you have there in that basket?
>
> Just a few loaves and some fish.

> Go ahead and give them what you have there.
>
> Jesus, You don't seem to understand—there are thousands out there—this will never be enough—don't You have any other ideas?
>
> No my child, just distribute what you have.
>
> I won't go, Jesus—I cannot face the crowd with what I have—I will look stupid.

How many of us would have responded like the boy in this fictitious account? Fortunately, the boy responded appropriately to Jesus' instruction. According to Scripture, he stepped out knowing full well that he did not have enough and Jesus miraculously increased what he had. God desires to use you and me in much the same way, if we will only step out. He is not looking for our sufficiency, He is looking for our obedience and availability.

4. Keep the End in View

We must remember that we are in this thing for the long haul. It is important to have a big picture or long-term view if we are to be successful. If we do not maintain this scope we will always be looking for the quick and temporary fixes to get us over the hump.

Having a healthy view about where we are headed can give us patience for the day-to-day grind. Let me use a golfing example. Don't get the wrong idea here. I am not a good golfer. In fact, the longest relationship I ever had with a golf ball was about twelve seconds. I hit the ball and then have to ask those around me if they know where it went.

In search of a little expertise, I have noticed one similarity among most serious golfers. They are meticulous about their approach to the game. They really check out the lay of the land, the wind conditions, distance, etc. They even ask others for advice on the selection of just the right club. Golfers know that the goal is to get through eighteen holes with the fewest strokes possible. Every decision that is made along the way will affect the final score. Therefore, every move is made with a great deal of thought and caution.

Why don't we take this same approach with life? Sometimes our husbands or wives need the putter and we have the driver out. Sometimes, just like in golf, you have to chip out from behind that obstacle and lose a stroke in order to realize the greater gain.

A Real Challenge

Three years ago, I flew into San Antonio, Texas. When I arrived at the airport, I went immediately to the rental car counter. While my paperwork was being processed, I was informed that my drivers license had expired and I would not be allowed to rent a car. So there I sat, a ministry leader ready to teach men how to appropriately respond to their circumstances as a Christian, and what did I do next? I immediately started thinking about how I could manipulate myself out of this predicament. "Maybe if I found someone who had a valid license and they rented the car for me," I thought. I even involved my office in trying to figure out some way to compromise.

Still tormented by my situation, I grabbed my considerable array of luggage and headed down the rental car corridor. Then the thought came to me, "Maybe if I go to a different counter and start again they won't notice that my license has expired." I even looked behind me and realized that there was a post protecting me from being seen by the previous sales associate.

I was almost through the paperwork when the new associate asked me for my license. I tried to distract her with a few jokes. But that did not work. She asked, "Do you have an extension for this license, Mr. D'Acchioli?"

"Why no, why?" "Sir, it expired three months ago," she replied. "You're kidding!" I will never forget what happened next. In this awkwardly quiet moment I heard the Lord speak to me, "What are you doing?" From my heart I knew what He meant. "I am sorry Lord, I obviously don't know what I am doing." I dragged my luggage to a nearby bench, sat down and had to choke back the tears. I felt ashamed. God had called upon me to communicate the importance of living a Christ-like life, and that day I chose to ignore His counsel with my lowly behavior.

If given the same circumstance, what would your reaction have been? Would you have responded in a similar manner? I am sorry, but if you and I are going to be true followers of Christ, we do not have that liberty. This may seem like a small compromise, but where do you draw the line?

The last several pages have outlined *four principles to make a difference*. Are they difficult to live by? You bet they are! But, they represent the difference between a Christianity that is considered political and self-righteous and one that is truly like Christ. We can no longer accept the former.

How Am I Doing?

Let me ask you, how are you doing?
Men, are you the Priests of your homes?
Do you love your wife as Christ loved the church?
Women, are you loving and committed wives?
Are you there for your family?
Do you compromise on even the insignificant things?
Do you love and serve those with whom you work?
Are you involved in your church?
Do you pray for those you do not like or agree with?

Why is all of this so important? It is because people are watching those of us who call ourselves Christians.

As I mentioned earlier, they are looking for the real deal. I once heard a well-known Christian leader tell about a time when he was making a long distance telephone call from a pay phone with the help of an operator. When he was finished, a bunch of quarters started pouring out of the phone. It was like a slot machine. He tried to stop them to no avail. They just kept coming. (I did not know this, but apparently the operator has remote control over this function.) Finally, he dialed zero and told the operator what was happening and asked what he should do. The operator said, "I know who you are sir, I just wanted to *see* what you would do." Even when we least suspect it, we are being observed!

What Would Your Neighbor Say about You?

I want to close this chapter with a story. Bill and Mary were a couple living in a downtown apartment complex in a somewhat rough part of town. They were not married and their lifestyle consisted of alcohol, drugs, and practically anything that would give them a sense of worldly pleasure. They knew nothing about God. Bill would often look out his apartment window and view the surrounding neighborhood. The people below were always fighting and yelling, and many times helicopters were circling overhead. But, there was one family that lived right behind Bill and Mary. Bill could easily observe their back yard from across the alley.

These people were different. In sharp contrast to the rest of the neighborhood, they never said anything unkind or raised their voices at each other. Instead they were always loving and considerate. Bill was somewhat perplexed by this behavior. Then one day while the family was away, their dog, (we'll call him Bowser) got into the trash and spread garbage all over the back yard. Bill thought to himself, "When this guy gets home I am finally going to see him lose it with this dog." He watched and waited.

A short time later, the family returned and this is what Bill witnessed. The man came out of the back door, looked down at Bowser, and in a soft tone said, "Oh Bowser," and proceeded to pick up the trash. That was it!

Bill was furious. He wanted to beat that dog himself. The next day Bill and Mary were walking down the street. They spotted the couple and walked over to them. Bill wanted to meet them and was warmed by their tender and polite response. After exchanging some small talk, the couple invited Bill and Mary over to their house for dinner. That Friday night, seated around the family dinner table, Bill and Mary accepted Jesus Christ as their personal Lord and Savior; all because they observed the unique and godly behavior of a neighbor.

So, what would your neighbor say about you?

Chapter Summary:

1. What we *do* is much more important than what we say.
2. As Christians, we are not called to judge, but rather to live a righteous life.
3. We need to have a healthy attitude toward those we do not like or agree with.
4. Jesus is not looking for our sufficiency—He is looking for our obedience.
5. It is time to get out of our comfort zone and begin to make a difference.

Discussion questions:

1. Think of a time when you tried to persuade someone with words. How successful were you? How did you feel?

2. How has this chapter affected your thinking about your approach with others?
3. Would you consider yourself a politically motivated Christian? Explain.

Write down one or two key ideas that you gleaned from this chapter and at least one new behavior you would like to start practicing.

Key Ideas

___

___

___

___

New Behavior/Commitment

___

___

___

___

Coming Up in Chapter Seven:

Chapter seven explores the need to maintain consistency in our life by establishing accountable relationships with others. In order for us to be effective we need each other for support and encouragement. We will discuss in great detail what the various options are for these important relationships by reviewing four *relationship systems.*

Chapter Seven

Staying the Course: Building Accountable Relationships

One of the largest living organisms on the planet is the Giant Redwood Tree, sometimes referred to as a Giant Sequoia. They are so large that tunnels have been carved through them for vehicles to pass through. Here is something you probably did not know about this marvel of nature. If you were able to select just one of these giants, uproot it, and take it anywhere in the world to transplant it in the strongest soil system you could find, it would not work. The slightest wind would blow it over. You see, the only way these enormous trees are able to stand is because their shallow root system is intertwined with other Giant Redwoods. They hold each other up.

Earlier, in the Introduction, I mentioned the three things that I discovered happy, secure, successful people had in common; they had an intimate relationship with God, an understanding of *how* and *why* God made them, and they were living the vision out. I want to share with you now a fourth ingredient that I have discovered these people have. They have come to understand the importance of maintaining consistency in life through accountable relationships with other people. Just like that Giant

Redwood, these people realize that the winds of the world are blowing more fiercely today than at any time in our history. If they are not connected, no matter how big and strong they may be, they will be blown over.

A Case for Accountability

There are two reasons for establishing accountable relationships. First, we need others in order to help us through life changing growth. Second, and of equal importance, is that we need others to help us to maintain that growth, to hold us accountable and to help us become more consistent. What I am about to discuss is not easy or popular to many in today's culture. We live in a world that has us so fractured and separated that many equate distance with safety. We don't want to get too close to others. After all, they may find out I am not what they think. This is a lie not only perpetrated by our culture, but by the devil himself. Have you ever repeated these words of condemnation? "Surely no one else struggles with this. I must be different."

Another reason we shy away from accountable relationships is that we are reluctant to enter into the painful and sometimes lengthy processes necessary for real change.

The Six Stages for Change

Our lives do not change simply because we attend an event, hear a good sermon, or read a great book. It would be nice if it worked that way, but evidence suggests that much more is needed if meaningful change is to take place in a person. I believe that there are six stages we must go through before *real* change can take place: EVENT, AWARENESS, DECISION, COMMITMENT, PROCESS, AND CHANGE. Let me give further clarification to each.

Event

An event can be anything from a PK rally, to reading a book, hearing a sermon, or even witnessing a wedding. My wife reminds me that a wedding is an event; it's not a marriage. Most of us want the event to produce the desired result. It would be quick and painless. "Let's get it over with." Unfortunately it does not work that way. The best an event can do is raise . . .

Awareness

Awareness often happens as the result of an event. I discover at a rally, seminar, or by reading a book that I need to get closer to God, pray more with my spouse, etc. This realization then leads to my making a . . .

Decision

I decide to do something about it. Here is a funny, example with which most of us can identify. It's New Years Eve. That is an EVENT. I have an AWARENESS that I am a little overweight and out of shape. I make a DECISION that, starting tomorrow, I am going to go on a diet and work out. New Year's day comes. The guys are all over for the games and my wife has made chili and garlic bread. I say to myself, "Well, I think I will start tomorrow." Then tomorrow comes and something else gets in the way. "Maybe Monday; that's it, Monday would be good." Meanwhile, six months later my belt buckle still has an un-obscured view of my shoes. Nothing has changed.

I call these first three stages the *cycle of hopelessness* (see chart page 125). I believe that is how most of us live. In order to break out of this situation we must press forward to the fourth stage . . .

Commitment

Commitment is the bridge that, if crossed, can transform the old man into the new. You may want to look up the difference between decision and commitment in the dictionary. It is powerful. Commitment is what it takes to enter into the most important and difficult stage of all . . .

Process

Here is where most of us struggle. What is process? It is behavioral change over a period of time. That means challenge and a level of intention that most of us are unwilling to enter into. For the most part, we are a people that are very impatient with anything having to do with process. We do not want to work for results if it means experiencing any kind of short-term discomfort. We have become what I like to call a *microwave generation,* filled with such accelerants as steroids, rapid weight loss diets, and get rich quick schemes. We often look for these same quick fixes to aid in our behavioral development. What many of us fail to understand is that God is really more interested in the process, the habits we form, and the way we live, than in any of our lofty goals.

Process is the only way to bring about lasting and meaningful . . .

Change

The desired result—an alteration in our behavior—a new and higher level of maturity.

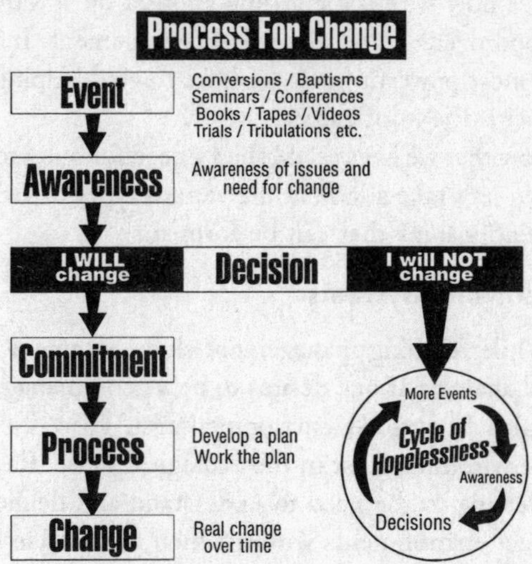

Because sometimes the process involved for change can be difficult, we need others who will pray, love, and encourage us through it. Once we are on the other side, we will need others to hold us accountable and help us maintain a steady course in order to stay consistent.

Prayer and Encouragement

Galatians 6:1-3 says, "Brothers, if someone is caught in a sin, you who are spiritual should restore him gently. But watch yourself, or you also may be tempted. Carry each other's burdens, and in this way you will fulfill the law of Christ."

This verse is a strong call to carry each other's burdens. The call is to pray and work through difficulties with each other. But I cannot carry your burdens if I do not know what they are. In other words, we must get to the point where we are willing to become transparent enough to share our burdens with each other.

The Bible also says in Hebrews 10:24, "And let us consider how we may spur one another on toward love and good deeds." We all need encouragement. It is one of the most powerful tools we have toward helping each other with life's difficulties.

Now that we have established a need for one another's support, let's take a look at the various types of accountable relationships that can be formed.

Relationship Systems

While teaching management skills, I came across a helpful analogy: If one desires to be a good manager one must also be a good environmentalist. Now I do not mean environmentalist in the ecological sense. Rather, I am referring to the need to understand and deliberately construct environments within which predictable things will happen.

Let's use a greenhouse as an example. We know that if we build an effective greenhouse, with just the right amount of light, moisture, etc. that we will see our plants thrive and grow. This same concept can also be applied to establishing accountable relationships. What I am suggesting is that we take into consideration our unique needs and then design a relationship system that will bring about the desired result.

Before I go any further, allow me to explain four different types of relationship systems. Of course there will be some variations on these, but I would like to stick to this guideline for the purpose of our discussion.

1. Discipleship / Mentor

Purpose: Spiritual growth and development for the one being discipled. (Gender specific)

Ideal Number: 2

Management: Mentor leads.

2. Fellowship / Social

Purpose: Meeting other Christians, building friendships and prayer support.
Ideal Number: 8-12
Management: Host or leader led.

3. Study / Informational

Purpose: Bible study or other structured learning systems designed to build knowledge.
Ideal Number: Open
Management: Study group leader.

4. Accountability / Encourager

Purpose: Prayer support, advice, encouragement and accountability. (Gender specific)
Ideal Number: 3-5
Management: Leaderless with some structure/questions.

As you can see, depending upon which of these you may want to join, the outcome or benefits will vary. At one time or another, I have been in all four of these. Today, I find myself committed to the fourth because I find that this kind of group or system best meets the needs of someone with the kind of schedule and demands that I am experiencing. I also find that the Accountability/Encourager group creates the best opportunity to find the kind of support that will help bring about real and sustained change in a person's life.

Let's focus on the third and fourth systems to further amplify what a given environment can produce. In the third Study/Informational model, which is designed to have a leader and work through a structured learning system, people will gain new information and become more knowledgeable. The tendency will be to stick to the structure or schedule in order to finish the weekly assignment. In the fourth Accountability/Encourager example, there is no such pressure. It is run without a leader and is much more spontaneous in format. This group is more likely to deal with private and personal issues and concerns than the former. It all depends upon your focus.

The Accountability Group Model

I want to spend the rest of this chapter talking about the fourth system, the Accountability/Encourager group. Perhaps you are already in or are planning to start one of the other relationship systems. If so, that is all right. You will still benefit from what I am about to discuss. I want to concentrate on this last model because I am convinced that it best meets the needs of most of us, especially those of us who desire to live out what God has revealed in this book.

As you read the following verses from Ezekiel, I would like you to pay special attention to the words I have chosen to italicize.

> I looked, and I saw a windstorm coming out of the north—an immense cloud with flashing lightning and surrounded by brilliant light. The center of the fire looked like glowing metal, and in the fire was what looked like *four* living creatures. In appearance their form was that of a man, but each of them had four faces and four wings. Their legs were *straight*; their feet were like those of a calf and *gleamed* like *burnished bronze*. Under their wings on their four sides they had the hands of a man. All four of them had faces and wings, *and their wings touched one another*. Each one went *straight ahead*; *they did not turn as they moved*. Their faces looked like this: Each of the four had the face of a *man*, and on the right side each had the face of a *lion*, and on the left the face of an *ox*; each also had the face of an *eagle*. Such were their

> faces. Their *wings were spread out upward*; each had two wings, one *touching the wing of another creature* on either side, and two wings covering its body. *Each one went straight ahead. Wherever the spirit would go, they would go, without turning as they went.* (Ezek. 1:4-12, emphasis added)

What an incredibly powerful picture of a potential accountability group. Four people, straight and burnished bronze, wings touching each other, focused straight ahead, a man, a lion, an ox, and an eagle, pointing up to heaven, going where the Spirit leads. I am particularly taken by the implications of the four different creatures and how they complement each other. It reminds me of what we discussed earlier in this book regarding the importance of our different gifts working together. If you took the time to study the strengths of the four individual beings in these verses, you would begin to understand the tremendous potential that they have in their unity. It is a strength that could never be achieved apart.

The Bible says in Proverbs 27:17, "As iron sharpens iron, so one man sharpens another." I believe that this process of sharpening refers to the development of four qualities in our life: consistency, stability, confidence, and significance. Let's look at what the dictionary has to say about each:

Consistent Holding always to the same principles or practice—in accord.

Stable The state or quality of being stable or fixed—firmness of character, purpose, or resolution. Steadfast.

Confident The fact of feeling or being certain—assurance.

Significant Having or expressing a meaning—full of meaning—important.

How Do I Begin?

If you desire to join or start your own accountability group, I suggest that you begin by asking the Lord to lead you to at least one other partner. Then, the two of you can begin meeting and praying for others to join. If you are already in one of these groups, the following information may help you better understand some of the dynamics and add to your current experience.

I want to share six criteria that you may want to consider before bringing people into your group. This criteria is best applied by answering the following questions:

1. Does this person love the Lord and desire a deeper relationship with Him? Keep in mind that this is not a discipleship group or a place to win over the unbeliever.
2. Will this person be *available*? This is the principle of commitment and priority. Will they attend every meeting? Will they be there for the other members of the group, night or day?
3. Will they be *accountable*? This is the principle of responsibility and confidentiality. Will they be diligent to pray and keep your secrets, no matter what?
4. Can they be *vulnerable*? This is the principle of transparency. Will they open up?
5. Are they *teachable*? A person can be available, accountable, and vulnerable, but if they are not teachable, they are not ready.
6. Finally, does this person bring balance to the group in terms of age, level of maturity, etc.? People tend to identify with those who may be in a similar place in life.

Before leaving this topic, I want to deliver two cautions. First, you should not consider relatives or co-workers for your group. Think about it. Where are the two areas in your life that you experience the most problems? That's right, at home and at work. You do not need that kind of dynamic. Second, and of critical importance, make sure that you are on solid ground with your spouse. If your husband or wife does not want you to join a group, don't. In a situation like this, you must first earn their trust. There was a time when my wife did not want me in an accountability group. Today, she is concerned if I am not in one. That transition did not take place over night. Talk it over and come to an understanding before you jump in.

Group Dynamics

The size of your accountability group may also contribute to the effectiveness of your meeting. I personally recommend between three and five members. Four is just about right. If you have more than five, it becomes too easy for some to hideout and not get involved. With fewer than four, you have the potential to cancel meetings because of schedules or other things that may get in the way of faithful attendance.

I would also recommend that you consider a leaderless management structure. I have found that when we come together as equals and enter into a time of sharing openly with each other that God has a way of orchestrating the meeting. Men and women will naturally take a leadership position according to the subject matter or the prompting of the Holy Spirit.

The only danger in this approach is the tendency to become superficial and overly social. In an effort to avoid this from happening, develop a set of mutually accepted questions that each member of your group has permission to ask at any time. These questions, if carefully selected, will quickly snap your group back to order. Here are some examples:

1. Have you prayed with your wife/husband this week?
2. How are you doing with your personal devotional times?
3. What temptations did you experience this week? Did you overcome?
4. Do you have any unforgiveness in your heart toward anyone?

It is not a bad idea to stop every three or four months and take stock of how everyone in the group thinks you are doing.

Covenants to Keep

One of the most remarkable men in history was John Wesley. Few men have influenced modern Christianity as profoundly as this man. Wesley created eight covenants that he applied to groups, or bands, as he called them. Living up to these covenants can greatly contribute to a positive group dynamic. I encourage you to photocopy these and distribute them to each member of your group.

1. The Covenant of Love (agape):
   Your commitment to each individual in your group must be of the spirit that says: "Nothing you do or say will make me stop loving you."
2. The Covenant of Availability:
   a. I will be available, when humanly possible, each time our group meets.
   b. I will make myself available to any member of our group whenever they are in need.
3. The Covenant of Prayer:
   I will pray for each member of our group consistently.
4. The Covenant of Confidentiality:
   Understanding that the other points in this covenant are only possible in the security of a trust relationship, I will, therefore, make the commitment to our group

to share *nothing* outside of our group that has been shared inside our group or shared in private ministry with another member of our group.

5. The Covenant of Openness:
Understanding that I cannot know you and that you cannot know me unless we tell each other who we are. I will make the commitment to tell you who I am, both in my strengths and in my weaknesses.
6. The Covenant of Sensitivity:
I will ask God to make me sensitive to the needs of each person in our group and I will consciously make the commitment to *listen* to each person each time they speak, whether in words, actions, or attitudes.
7. The Covenant of Honesty:
Understanding that "speaking the truth in love" is both positive and constructive unto bodily growth. I will allow God to use me in our group's growth process by telling you when I agree and when I disagree.
8. The Covenant of Accountability:
It is my conviction that God has placed me in our group for building up the Body of Christ, and that from time to time, within our group, it will be necessary for me to seek the mind of the Lord through the counsel and advice of our group. I will accept the responsibility for their counsel and advice and report to them what I have done with their collective wisdom.

Thank You, Dear Friend

I want to thank you for taking the time to read this book. I am both humbled and honored. What you have just read represents a passion that the Lord has been developing in me over the past ten years or so. It is a passion to see people understand *how* and *why* God made them and become successful at living out a victorious life. I encourage you to commit to the principles you have discovered.

I want to close with excerpts taken from the writings of Oswald Chambers in his wonderful and timeless work, *My Utmost for His Highest*:

> "Rivers of Living Water"—*John 7:38*
>
> A river touches places of which its source knows nothing, and Jesus says if we have received His fullness, however small the visible measure of our lives, out of us will flow the rivers that will bless to the uttermost parts of the earth. We have nothing to do with the outflow—"This is the work of God that ye *believe*. . . ." God rarely allows a soul to see how great a blessing He is.
>
> A river is victoriously persistent, it overcomes all barriers. For a while it goes steadily on its course, then it comes to an obstacle and for a while it is balked, but it soon makes a pathway round the obstacle. Or a river will drop out of site for miles, and presently emerge again broader and grander than ever. You can see God using some lives, but into your life an obstacle has come and you do not seem to be of any use. Keep paying attention to the Source, and God will either take you round the obstacle or remove it. The river of the Spirit of God overcomes all obstacles. Never get your eyes on the obstacle or on the difficulty. The obstacle is a matter of indifference to the river

which will flow steadily through you if you remember to keep right at the Source. Never allow anything to come between yourself and Jesus Christ, no emotion, or experience; nothing must keep you from the one great sovereign Source.

Think of the healing and far-flung rivers nursing themselves in our souls! God has been opening up marvelous truths to our minds, and every point He has opened up is an indication of the wider power of the river He will flow through us. If you believe in Jesus, you will find that God has nourished in you mighty torrents of blessing for others.

There is only one relationship that matters, and that is your relationship to a personal Redeemer and Lord. Let everything else go, but maintain that at all costs, and God *will* fulfill His purpose through your life. One individual life may be of priceless value to God's purposes, and you may be that life.

Chapter Summary:

1. Accountability is the key to consistency.
2. There are at least four different kinds of *relationship systems*. Selecting the right one for your need is important.
3. Members of my group need to be *available, accountable, vulnerable, and teachable.*

Discussion Questions:

1. How do you feel about being accountable to others?
2. Describe a time where you experienced the *cycle of hopelessness*?
3. What kind of *relationship system* would best suit you, and why?

Write down one or two key ideas that you gleaned from this chapter and at least one new behavior you would like to start practicing.

Key Ideas

____

____

____

____

New Behavior/Commitment

____

____

____

____

A Final Word to the Doubter

Perhaps you, like so many, have come this far in your search for meaning and purpose and are still having difficulty believing God is real. You have read this book, find many of the things we have discussed interesting, but you still have your doubts. You are not abnormal. We live in a world today that says *I'll believe it when I see it*. I want to suggest to you that just maybe *you will see it when you believe*. This is what faith is all about, accepting something even when it does not square with some of our preconceived notions.

After a recent event, a man who was struggling over God's existence challenged me. To him, nothing seemed to make sense. He needed some scientific evidence. I immediately resonated with this man, having found myself in the very same quandary several years back. I asked him if he remembered, perhaps as a little boy lying in bed, looking up at the stars and pondering the vastness of the universe. He said, of course. I continued, "Can you comprehend the idea of there being no end?"

"No," he said. "I don't think anyone can." He is right. It is difficult to comprehend there being no end to space. But, scientifically there can't be. Think about it. If there were an end, what would be on the other side?

As mind-boggling as this is, think about the opposite. Is there such a thing as too small? Many scientists today are saying that there can't be. After all, when you develop a microscope powerful enough to see the smallest particle known to man, you are still left with the question of what that particle is made up of. I don't think there can be "too small."

One could also consider the concept of time. It has always been and always will be. Modern science cannot explain any of these phenomena with any degree of certainty. Yet, as a society we accept these ideas with a strange mixture of scientific theory and faith. So why is it that we so easily accept these notions, but have difficulty believing that there may be a Designer/Creator for our universe; a God who has no beginning and no end?

If this is not enough to get you thinking, let me throw a little science into the formula. Edwin Yamauchi, professor of history at Miami University asserts that there is more documented evidence to substantiate the fact that Jesus Christ lived, than any other religious founder in history. Did you know that the scientific odds of all of the Old Testament prophecies of the coming Lord being fulfilled in one person are impossible and yet they were all fulfilled in Jesus? Did you know that many scientists, using their own formulas, now admit that evolution is *not* possible? An abundance of scientific evidence is available if you are interested in doing a bit of research. A great resource for further study is a book by Josh McDowell, *New Evidence That Demands A Verdict,* Thomas Nelson Publishing.

Please understand what I am saying, because the consequences are serious. If God is real, if you and I have been created for eternity, if the message of salvation is true, that we must accept Him in order to have eternal life, if heaven and hell really do exist, why take a chance? You and I have been offered the greatest gift in the universe, and it is available to you and me by simply applying a seed of faith. Approach God as a child approaches his/her parent and simply ask Him to come into your heart. You have absolutely nothing to lose and *everything* to gain. You and I have the privilege of drawing near to God anytime and anywhere. Why not do it right now?

God's grace is sufficient to free you from the bondages of your past, to wash away all of your sin and guilt, to make you a new creation in Christ. Scripture says that Jesus loves us with an unconditional and everlasting love, so much so that He was willing to lay down His own life on the cross so that you and I might live and have eternal life. He made the ultimate sacrifice for you! Accept His promises, accept His forgiveness, *accept Him,* and I promise that you will soon have a powerful and life-altering experience!

Are you ready to begin a new life in Christ? If so, let me suggest the following prayer: *Lord, I know that I am a sinner. I realize that nothing I do can save me, but it is Your grace. I believe You are real and I want to ask You to come into my heart right now. I want to accept You as my personal Lord and Savior.*

If you just recited the words above with sincerity and conviction—welcome! You have just made the single most significant decision of your life. As a new follower of Christ, I pray that you will seriously consider the principles that I have outlined in this book. Do not hesitate to apply what you have discovered. *Nothing* will bring a greater sense of fulfillment to your life than knowing Christ and coming to a full understanding of *how* and *why* He made you.

Finally, if you have just made a first time commitment to the Lord, would you allow me the honor and privilege of helping you get started in your new journey? If you will write or E-mail me that you have accepted Jesus, I promise that I will respond with some free information and resources to help you get started in your new life. You can write Vince D'Acchioli, *On Target Ministries,* P.O. Box 1654, Monument CO, 80132-1654. Or you can E-mail me at vince@otm.org.

God bless you,

Vince

Philippians 3:13-14

How Am I Wired?

Discover Your Natural Gifts (From Chapter Three)

> We have different gifts, according to the grace given us. If a man's gift is prophesying, let him use it in proportion to his faith. If it is serving, let him serve; if it is teaching, let him teach; if it is encouraging, let him encourage; if it is contributing to the needs of others, let him give generously; if it is leadership, let him govern diligently; if it is showing mercy, let him do it cheerfully (Rom. 12:6-8, NIV).

Instructions:

Read each statement and determine whether it describes you using the scale below. When finished, add up each section and refer to the instructions at the end for scoring.

0 = **not** me	3 = **usually** like me
1 = **little** like me	4 = **mostly** like me
2 = **sometimes** like me	5 = **always** like me

*Red*______________________

___ Seems to have no fear
___ Does not yield to what others think
___ Has a strong will
___ Prefers verbal expression over written
___ May exaggerate in order to convince
___ Is an absolutist *(all is black or white)*
___ Their frankness may appear harsh
___ Is usually found where the action is
___ At times appears provocative and radical
___ Does not like compromise
___ Is courageous and able to stand alone
___ At times appears to thrive on confrontation
___ Can be inflexible and opinionated
___ Is a leader, sometimes a crusader
___ Can withstand pain, stress and persecution

_____ **Section Total**

*White*____________________

___ Is able to detect and meet needs of others
___ Willingly performs any task that needs to get done
___ Most easily learns by doing
___ Will inconvenience self to meet others needs
___ More readily expresses love by doing
___ Is very flexible
___ May interfere with development of others
___ Enjoys practical people and organizations
___ Enjoys working with physical projects
___ Is usually a good worker and follower
___ May appear to have an independent spirit because of their insistence on serving
___ Often lets people take advantage of them
___ Eagerness can be read as ambition
___ Reacts to non-helpers in practical ways
___ Tends to be practical in all areas of life

_____ **Section Total**

*Blue*______________________

___ Likes research to discover full meaning for personal benefit
___ Enjoys checking out new information
___ Often clarifies by giving opposing views
___ Loves words and definitions
___ Teaches as a method for problem solving
___ Tends to present themselves logically
___ Is diligent and thorough
___ Retains and organizes large numbers of facts
___ Will test the knowledge of others
___ Usually objective and may appear insensitive
___ Tends to give detailed instructions
___ May appear to think they are always right
___ Can appear to be overly critical with a desire to correct misinformation
___ Develops self-control and discipline at a young age
___ Appears to have a stable personality

_____ **Section Total**

*Green*______________________

___ Able to choose words that encourage
___ Enjoys utilizing life principles from stories
___ Makes others feel good about themselves just by being around them
___ May shirk work to talk with others
___ Can encourage others regardless of personal circumstances
___ Needs company of others on regular basis
___ Enjoys one-on-one sharing and counseling
___ Personalizes most reading material
___ Consistently expresses enthusiasm
___ Patient with involved problems
___ Behavior usually consistent and dependable
___ Willing to go the extra mile with people

___ Can become more involved with the problem than the person
___ Prefers reading and teaching materials which have practical examples
___ Shares personal insights in meaningful and helpful ways

______ **Section Total**

*Orange*____________________

___ Uses their material goods efficiently
___ Enjoys giving to unpublicized needs
___ Receives great pleasure from giving
___ Creative in discovering resources
___ Tends to give of their best
___ Prefers monetary involvement with organizations
___ Can limit other's opportunity to give to them
___ Wants their gifts to have lasting benefits
___ Tends away from all indebtedness
___ Will make personal sacrifices in order to give
___ Prefers supportive behind-the-scenes role
___ Appears to have a *(worldly)* value system
___ Functions well with a little or a lot
___ May appear to be trying to control through their giving
___ Appreciates and is sensitive to gratefulness

______ **Section Total**

*Purple*____________________

___ Able to visualize and integrate tasks, projects, and people into common goals
___ Able to maximize talents of others
___ Avoids involvement in areas that are not theirs
___ Will assume responsibility if no one else does
___ Prefers planning vs develop-as-you-go

___ Will delegate whenever possible
___ Tends to be neat and orderly in personal life
___ Able to endure reaction from others to accomplish the goal in time
___ Enjoys helping others become more efficient
___ Looks for new challenge when projects are completed
___ Can finalize difficult decisions
___ May appear to be a perfectionist
___ Can appear to use people because of a tendency to view them as resources
___ Can seem insensitive or callous because of their drive
___ Is firm and steadfast regardless of opposition
______ **Section Total**

*Yellow*______________________

___ Able to identify with those in distress
___ Tends to be an empathetic listener
___ Their empathy may feed others' self pity
___ Will give up personal rights for others
___ Tends to be easily hurt and is sensitive to words or actions that offend others
___ Desires to support and protect
___ Is humble and strongly reacts to pride
___ Can't withstand stress and personal attacks
___ Reacts negatively to people who seem callous
___ Tends to be guided by emotions
___ Likes to be around people socially
___ Weeps easily
___ Lacks firmness and may appear indecisive
___ Desires harmony and will compromise for it
___ Avoidance of confrontation may be viewed as weakness
______ **Section Total**

Instructions:

Add up your points for each section and fill in your top two scores/colors in the spaces provided below. Refer to the table marked CODE to find the associated gift.

Top
Score #_____ Color_________ Gift________

Second
Score #_____ Color_________ Gift________

CODE:

Red = Perceiver	White = Ministry
Blue = Teaching	Green = Exhorting
Orange = Giving	Purple = Administration
Yellow = Mercy	

Application:

This test was designed to help you better understand the way God has made you. Your *natural gifts*, (sometimes referred to as your *bent* or *temperament)*, become the filter through which you see life, and can have a strong influence on the decisions you make.

By rereading the statements in your two top score categories you are simply looking at the behavioral characteristics associated with people who have those gifts.

We recommend that you share this information with your family, pastor and other friends and begin looking for opportunities to enter into activities that will maximize your gifts.

For instance, if you score high in *administration* or *perceiver*, look for projects to manage. If you are more into the *ministry* or *mercy* areas, you may want to take a missions trip or visit a hospital. Many times in the exercising of your *natural gifts,* God reveals His great purpose for your life.

Finally, this device is not intended to suggest a career path, or to influence you to change your vocation. It simply suggests that, whatever your vocation is, you will approach it within the context of your *natural gifts*. If you happen to be searching for a new vocation, this information can be helpful as it gives you some ideas about your temperament. Listed below are the *Natural Gifts* and some suggested vocations that best fit them.

Please keep in mind that this is a very loose association and does not take into consideration your personal likes and dislikes with regard to various lines of work.

Hard-sided Gifts: (logical—organized—structured)
Perceiver—Teacher—Administration

Soft-sided Gifts: (sensitive—desires to help—give)
Ministry—Mercy—Giving—Exhorting

Perceiver

Perceivers are perceptive people. These are the kind of people you want to be around in an emergency. They can process a lot of information quickly and get to the-meat-of-the-matter. They will usually gravitate to the highest and best course of action.

They generally make good leaders but depending upon their second gift they may either possess a dictatorial management style or more of a team approach. Perceivers whose second gift is on the hard-side will tend to be more autocratic, while those whose second gift leans toward the soft-side will be more democratic.

Vocational Ideas:

Air traffic controller—pilot—detective work—lawyer—counselor—salesperson—analyst—military officer—emergency medical—teaching—management/leadership—consultant—board member—business owner—developer

Ministry

If you have the gift of ministry, you are a natural helper. You love to help people in need. People who possess this gift usually make excellent employees. They tend to be very practical and enjoy physical labor where results are easy to see. They take great satisfaction from completing projects.

If your second gift is on the soft-side you may lack some organizational skills but your sensitivity to people will be very strong. If your second gift is on the hard-side you will tend to be a little more organized and calculating.

Vocational Ideas:

Factory worker—planning—architect—builder—cab/bus driver—civil servant—day care—sales associate—cook—computer programmer—farming—flight attendant—designer—librarian—nursing—mechanic—hair stylist/grooming—office worker—book keeper—secretary/reception—teacher—waiter/waitress

Teaching

Teachers love to organize and structure things. They tend to be very logical and enjoy discovering and communicating facts. They also love to create environments where others can learn. Teachers love to research and will usually challenge the ideas of others by asking a lot of questions.

If a teacher's second gift is on the hard-side it can cause them to be overly critical and domineering. It can also be a great asset for no-nonsense approaches to tasks or problems. If the second gift is on the soft-side it can sometimes bring a nice balance when dealing with people on a personal level.

Vocational Ideas:

Professor/teacher—lab research—programmer—doctor/medical technician—analyst—pastor—journalist—scientist—pharmacy—psychologist/psychiatrist—news reporter—administration—legal work/lawyer

Exhorting

Exhorters are often referred to as encouragers. People with this gift will tend to look for and find the best in others. They tend to be patient and love long conversations where they can get to know others. They also love to share personal experiences as a form of encouragement and counsel.

Exhorting will usually have a soft-sided second gift associated with it. They make wonderful coaches and counselors and enjoy helping bring out the best in people. Unless the second gift is on the hard-side they do not generally make good managers/leaders. A great combination for leadership is exhorting combined with *perceiver* or *administration.*

Vocational Ideas:

Counselor—coach—personnel work—public relations—real estate—therapist—radio/TV personality—social work—travel guide—ministry work/pastor—receptionist—advertising agent—personal agent—lawyer

Giving

People who posses the gift of *giving* can freely give of their time or resources without ever having to be recognized for it. They love to give. They are both creative and practical in their accumulation and management of resources.

The gift of *giving* associated with another soft-sided gift usually produces people who will freely give to a cause without having to be intimately involved with the end result. This same gift combined with the hard-side will produce someone who is just as free to give, but usually wants an accounting of the outcome.

Vocational Ideas:

Auditor—banker—bookkeeper—business owner—buyer—investor—financial consultant—office worker—emergency response—teacher—sales associate—waiter/waitress—mechanical work

Administration

Administrators are very organized. If you were to walk into their closet you would likely see all of the clothes neatly arrayed. They may have a tendency toward efficiency at the expense of effectiveness. When given a task they become highly focused on getting it done.

When this gift is associated with another hard-sided gift, it can produce people who are so structured that no amount of gray area can be tolerated. These are the kind of people who make great turnaround management specialists. They have little time or patience with mediocre work. When this gift is complemented with one on the soft-side it usually produces strong general-management skills. They can be firm and organized yet inspire people to follow them.

Vocational Ideas:

Teacher/professor—business executive—business owner—entrepreneur—store manager—contractor—lawyer—marketing—politician—producer—department manager—legal assistant—sales associate—business or school administration—team captain

Mercy

Mercy is the softest of the soft-sided gifts. These are people who are ultra sensitive to other people's pain and need. They tend to be very emotional and make excellent listeners. They also have a difficult time identifying with overly aggressive people.

Most often this gift has another soft-sided gift associated as the number two. In this case it indicates a high level of relational skill with some weakness in the organizational areas. Those who possess strong *mercy* gifts generally do not do well with deadlines or projects that need a lot of timeline management. If, however there is a hard-sided gift associated it can bring balance in the area of managing tasks.

Vocational Ideas:

Artist—writer/composing—nursing—childcare—musician—office worker—teacher—waiter/waitress—therapist—photography—hair stylist/grooming—sales associate

A Great Resource for a More In-Depth Study

For additional information and resources about discovering your natural gifts refer to: *Discovering Your God-Given Gifts,* by Don and Katie Fortune, Chosen Books. To order contact:

Heart to Heart Ministries,
P.O. Box 101, Kingston, WA 98364
#360-297-8878—www.heart2heart.org

The Wired to Work

Thirty-Day Action Plan

This thirty-day action plan has been designed to help develop a deeper relationship with God, a greater understanding of *how* and *why* He made you, and how to live a life that *will* make a difference.

It has been structured in a way that incorporates a precept-upon-precept approach. I am convinced that we need to introduce process driven strategies into our life if we are to realize *real* and *sustained* growth.

There are several ways in which this material can be used. It could be a daily reading incorporated into your devotional time—a weekly study—or used as a resource for your small group to work through. Here are some ideas for each:

Daily Reading

Keep this with your Bible and other devotional materials and make it a part of your daily reading.

Require of yourself to do a further study on the subject by looking up other verses or ideas—perhaps with the help of a concordance or Bible dictionary.

Make a note to yourself regarding what you intend to do differently in the *action plan* section and refer to it often.

Weekly Study

Because some of this material can be very challenging, you may want to read a volume once a week in order to give yourself more time to process the life application issues.

Enter a more in-depth time of study.

List the new behaviors or actions you intend to enter into over the next week—be specific.

Small Group Resource

This action plan is a great resource for your small group to study and discuss during your scheduled meetings.

You can all agree on what life application principle you each want to live out and then share the list with each other so that you can hold each member accountable.

You may want to make strategic commitments along the way and give everyone permission to check on each other's progress.

However you may choose to use this resource, may God richly bless you in the process.

Wired to Work Action Plan

Volume 1

Today's Verse/Thought: "Releasing the Past"

"Therefore, if anyone is in Christ, he is a new creation; the old has gone, the new has come!" *2 Cor. 5:17*

Life Implication:

The Bible makes it clear that we need to let go of our past. If we don't it will become a powerful stumbling block toward our discovering God's unique plan for our life. First John 2:11 warns us that if we hate our brother we will be in the darkness (in a fog, not able to see). The two biggest problem areas here are the hurts from past failures or negative experiences and unforgiveness toward others.

Life Application: (What I Must *Do*)

With regard to past failure, meditate on Isaiah 43:18-19, "Forget the former things; do not dwell on the past. See, I am doing a new thing! Now it springs up; do you not perceive it? I am making a way in the desert and streams in the wasteland."

Make a list right now of the negative influences from your past. Now, ask God to take them from you in prayer. At this point you must have the faith to believe that it is gone, over with, and be like Paul in Philippians 3 when he says, "Forgetting what is behind, I press on toward the mark." Pray every day until you feel God has released you.

Next, ask God to show you where you may be unforgiving. If you ask Him, He will. Then, DO IT! Decide to go to that person and do whatever you must to be reconciled. I promise you that you will experience a freedom like never before. Remember that God loves that person just as much as He loves you, no matter WHAT they may have done or said.

If the one you are having difficulty with is deceased or not able to be found, that matters little to God. He can still free you, but you MUST give it to Him.

Now you need to write down what you have just done and keep it with your devotional materials as a reminder. Remember that overcoming is not an event, it's a process.

Finally, remember that there will be times when your flesh and the devil will want to remind you how much you are a victim. Resist and remember that God is in control.

Action Plan

____

____

____

____

____

____

____

____

____

____

____

____

____

Wired to Work Action Plan
Volume 2

Today's Verse/Thought: "Resisting Temptations"

"Now that you have purified yourselves by obeying . . ." *1 Peter 2:12*

Life Implication:

The above verse suggests an incredible idea regarding the relationship between purification and obedience. The Bible is filled with scriptures admonishing us to *obey*. Proverbs 21:3 states, "to *do* what is right and just is more acceptable to the Lord than sacrifice." The Lord is calling us toward *righteousness* in order for us to be conformed to the likeness of His Son. In 1 Peter 3:11-12 the Bible says that God's ears are attentive to the prayers of a *righteous* man. Could it be that our difficulty getting closer to God may have a lot to do with our not ridding ourselves of the overt sin in our life? I think so!

Life Application: (What I Must *Do*)

What are the one or two temptations that most hinder you? Be honest with your response here. Make a commitment to overcome these obstacles. Understand what is at stake. It's ultimately your ability to get close to God in order to see His plan for your life.

The Apostle Paul in 1 Corinthians 9:24-27 talks about how he must *beat his body* in order to make it his slave. In Daniel 1:8 it says that Daniel *resolved* not to defile himself. In the New King James the word resolved is translated, *purposed in his heart*. In other words, Daniel had moral courage, he just said NO!

That is what we need to do. Refuse to be a victim and buy into the world and what it says is okay—the devil and what he wants us to do—and most importantly our own flesh. The Bible says in James 4:8 that if we will resist the devil he will flee from us.

After you have listed your points of struggle I suggest that you share them with your small group or a trusted friend or counselor. Give them permission to check on you and hold you accountable. You should also add them to your daily prayer list. Bring them before God every day.

Finally, the next time you are entertaining that thought or negative behavior, start speaking the name of Jesus. Just start to praise Him and you will not believe how fast that temptation goes away. My friend, it's a CHOICE! Make the right one and avoid the negative consequences.

Action Plan

Wired to Work Action Plan
Volume 3

Today's Verse/Thought: "Letting Go of My Way"

"Whoever finds his life will lose it, and whoever loses his life for my sake will find it." *Matthew 10:29*

Life Implication:

Probably the biggest single obstacle to getting close to God is our unwillingness to let Him into every part of our life. In Psalm 16:8 it says, "I have set the Lord *always* before me . . ." Because we live in a culture that teaches us that *what* we do is an indicator of *who* we are, we have turned the "I-can-do-it-myself" mentality into an art form. Unless we are willing to admit our absolute poverty to do anything without God, and go to Him for everything, we will never have the kind of relationship with Him that we desire.

Life Application: (What I Must *Do*)

In 2 Corinthians 12:7-11 we find Paul complaining about his thorn or weakness. God tells him that His power is made perfect in weakness, a foreign concept, but one that we must grasp. Recognize today that you are weak and decide to let God into every aspect of your life.

Make it a habit to pray about everything, not just the big or overwhelming obstacles. Pray before making that phone call or attending that meeting. Our Lord loves us and would never consider something too mundane for Him to be involved.

Make a list of the areas in your life where you have felt the need to be in control. Talk about them with your spouse or another close friend or counselor. Make it a point of daily prayer to offer your will to God in exchange for His. Every time you are about to make a decision remember to quietly ask God for guidance.

Action Plan

Wired to Work Action Plan
Volume 4

Today's Verse/Thought: "Knowing God"

"Come near to God and He will come near to you." *James 4:8*

Life Implication:

The secret to everything in life is a close personal relationship with God. You will never discover *how* and *why* God made you unless you are willing to get close to Him. Most of us stumble through life tripping over obstacles that we would not encounter were we to allow God to illuminate them. The reason why many do not go to God is because they really do not *know* Him. Here is the formula: You will never *rely* upon someone you do not *trust*, and you will never trust someone you do not *know*. Truly knowing God is the secret to a happy, secure and fulfilled life.

Life Application: (What I Must *Do*)

In Mark 12:30 the Bible admonishes us to love the Lord with all of our *heart, soul, mind* and *strength.* Ask yourself right now if you are missing the mark here.

Realize that you can't get to know someone who you are unwilling to spend time with. Decide today to get to know God. Make a commitment to spend time alone with Him every day. Be careful not to fall into the trap that says because I went to church today, or attended that Bible study, I have done my "God-thing." You can't develop intimacy in a crowd. You can't *really* get to know someone unless you get alone with him or her.

Get yourself a good Bible, devotional, (I like Oswald Chambers, *My Utmost for His Highest*) and a journal where you can write down what you believe God may be saying. Begin to use them every day.

I recommend you find a read through the Bible in a year program. It only takes fifteen to twenty minutes a day and takes you through the entire Scripture. Determine the time of day that you would like to spend with God and protect it diligently. Do not become legalistic. If you miss a day, don't worry about it. Get back on track tomorrow.

The next nine action plans will help you to form some solid habits in this area. They will discuss the importance of *reading* the Word, *praying* and *praising* God.

Action Plan

Wired to Work Action Plan
Volume 5

Today's Verse/Thought: "Finding a Quiet Place"

"One of those days Jesus went out to a mountainside to pray, and spent the night praying to God." *Luke 6:12*

Life Implication:

In the above verse, Jesus knew that it was not possible to have an intimate fellowship and communion with His Father without finding a quiet place. The same is true with us. We must have a place where we can be alone with God. A place where there are no worldly distractions. If you do not find a quiet place it will be almost impossible to concentrate on His Word, or pray and hear God speak to you.

Life Application: (What I Must *Do*)

Identify a place either in your home or somewhere where there is little chance that someone will interrupt you. Make sure that family members or others who may be around know and respect your privacy. If there are phones, unplug them. Make it as comfortable as possible.

Next, place your devotional materials where you can easily and comfortably access them. I like to surround myself with dictionaries and various commentaries so that I can easily look things up. I also keep my laptop and Bible software handy.

Action Plan

____

____

____

____

Wired to Work Action Plan
Volume 6

Today's Verse/Thought: "Having a Quiet Mind"

"The mind of sinful man is death, but the mind controlled by the Spirit is life and peace." *Romans 8:6*

Life Implication:

One of the most difficult challenges in life today is having a quiet mind. We live in a world that is sending out information so fast that it is impossible to keep up. The result of all of this is sometimes called "information overload." Confusion often sets in as we attempt to process all of this data. The twenty-first century mind is packed with more ideas and thoughts than it can reasonably process. Because time is such an important commodity we find ourselves thinking about several different ideas all at the same time. A good example of this is trying to listen to someone while at the same time thinking about something else you have to do.

One of the major reasons why we do not hear from God has to do with our preoccupation with unrelated thoughts. If we cannot quiet our minds and hearts and get into a state of neutral we will never hear God.

Life Application: (What I Must *Do*)

Whenever I find myself unable to quiet my mind I simply begin to praise Him. Praise is not complicated. We will discuss it in greater detail later. For now, try this. Just begin to talk to God. Tell Him how much you love Him. Thank Him for being who He is and for all that He has and is doing in your life.

Ask God directly to help you to quiet your mind and concentrate on Him. Tell Him how much you desire to hear His voice today.

Action Plan

Wired to Work Action Plan
Volume 7

Today's Verse/Thought: "The Power of Praise"

"The trumpeters and singers joined in unison, as with one voice, to give praise and thanks to the LORD. Accompanied by trumpets, cymbals and other instruments, they raised their voices in praise to the LORD and sang: "He is good; His love endures forever."

Then the temple of the LORD was filled with a cloud." *2 Chronicles 5:13*

Life Implication:

The above verse reminds us that God entered the temple as the direct result of His people praising Him. In the old covenant God would come into a physical place. The good news for us today is that God now resides in our heart. This incredible verse has so much more meaning today. As we praise Him, He comes into our very being.

There is a linkage between praising God and hearing His voice. Praise is mentioned in 319 verses in the bible. It is one of the most often mentioned ideas, yet one of the most misunderstood. God desires worship and praise more then any other thing we can do. He knows that the only way we can truly praise Him is to set ourselves aside . . . leaving room for Him to move into our lives. It creates a highway that leads to discovering His wonderful plans for us.

Praising God is the only way that we can overcome self and get closer to Him. In James 4:8 the bible says that if we draw near to God—He will draw near to us. Nothing brings us closer to God than praise. If we fail to develop an ongoing habit of praising God then we miss a major connection point with Him.

Life Application: (What I Must *Do*)

In the previous volume about quieting our minds we touched on this most important subject of praise. Let's now endeavor to make praise a daily habit. Even before you begin your reading or prayer time—just start to praise Him. Praise is not difficult. Verbalize your love for Him. Tell Him what a good God He is and how much you appreciate knowing Him.

Open the book of Psalms and read aloud verses that praise the Lord. You could even try singing verses from the Psalm to Him. Remember that God doesn't care how well you can carry a tune. He loves your praises—it is a sweet, sweet sound in His ear. After you praise Him for a while it is a good idea to just be quiet and listen for His voice. I find that He often talks to me just after I have spent time praising Him.

Action Plan

____

____

____

____

____

____

____

____

____

____

____

Wired to Work Action Plan
Volume 8

Today's Verse/Thought: "Reading the Word"

"Do not let this book of the law depart from your mouth; meditate on it day and night, so that you may be careful to do everything written in it. Then you will be prosperous and successful." *Joshua 1:8*

Life Implication:

The Bible makes it clear that we need to be reading the Word if we are going to be prosperous and successful. We must be careful not to equate what the Bible means as prosperous with earthly possessions or money. *Real* prosperity comes in understanding the depths of God and ultimately what He wants for our life. Psalm 119:105 says that the Word of God will be a lamp to my feet and a light to my path. If we are not reading the Word we are not realizing the potential for God to illuminate our daily steps and shine His wonderful beacon on the end of our path.

Life Application: (What I Must *Do*)

There is a difference between *reading* God's Word and *studying* the Bible. With the use of a read through the Bible in a year scheduling system you will do just that—*read* through the Bible. This is a good habit to form in order to fill yourself up with God's word.

When you *read* the Bible I suggest having a pen and paper at hand to record significant scripture verses that may awaken something in you. I like to underline them in my Bible and then go back later and re-read them.

Studying the Bible means that you are taking a verse, series of verses, or maybe a whole chapter or book and going more in-depth. You may want to separate your *reading* from your *study.* If you are in a Bible study with others you may not sense a need to do more. If not, I suggest that you pick a book and conduct a personal study with the use of your Bible dictionaries and concordances.

Finally, do not be discouraged if you find yourself reading a whole chapter and then not remembering what you just read. It is not uncommon. Just press on and read it anyway. Before you know it, you will have developed a long-lasting hunger for God's Word. Remember what goes in will eventually come out.

Action Plan

____

____

____

____

____

____

____

____

____

____

____

____

____

____

____

Wired to Work Action Plan
Volume 9

Today's Verse/Thought: "Purposeful Prayer"

"After they prayed, the place where they were meeting was shaken. And they were all filled with the Holy Spirit and spoke the Word of God boldly." *Acts 4:31*

Life Implication:

Prayer is the most wonderful privilege we have. It is communication with God. God responds to our prayers, and as He does, we develop the kind of progressive faith that brings us closer to Him. If you are not praying, your life will not work right. This is a fact. Prayer needs to become such a natural part of our life that it is like breathing. If you are a parent, you need to take that responsibility seriously and be praying for your kids every day.

Life Application: (What I Must *Do*)

Make a commitment right now to develop a healthy prayer habit. Determine when the best time of day would be. Some may be more alert in the morning. Others may find the evening to be more convenient.

Sit down and make a list of all of the things you would like to pray about. They will usually fall into categories like, family, friends, neighbors, vocational issues, etc. You may even want to separate your list into these categories.

Entries such as family members and major struggles and challenges you may want to carry across every day. Others could be on a once a week basis.

Once you have finished your list now is the time to divide it into manageable chunks. You can do this on your computer with a spreadsheet program or on a piece of paper. Write down the seven days of the week as column headings. Then break down your list into things that you will pray for on each of the days.

This exercise will help you focus on specific concerns each day. I find myself continually adding and subtracting requests. Don't be intimidated by long lists, the longer the better. You will never run out of things to pray about, and before you know it, you will begin to see answers!

Action Plan

Wired to Work Action Plan
Volume 10

Today's Verse/Thought: "Seeking Him First . . . Not What I Want"

"But seek first His kingdom and His righteousness, and all these things will be given to you as well." *Matthew 8:33*

Life Implication:

How would you like it if your kids or others who are close to you only came to you when they wanted something? I know you have probably experienced that. How does that make you feel? Do you think that our heavenly Father would feel any different? The Bible says that He is a jealous God who yearns for our attention and love.

Could it be that many of our requests go unanswered because we are asking in the wrong way? God loves us and knows what we need even before we ask. His real desire is for us to go to Him just because we love Him. If the only time you go to God is when you want something you will be greatly disappointed.

Life Application: (What I Must *Do*)

Seek the Giver of the gift—not the gift. Seek the face of God—not the hand of God. Try to remember the feelings you have when that little child or puppy or kitten crawls up in your lap just because they want to be near you. Now, do that with your heavenly Father. Just crawl up in His lap and begin to talk with Him. Tell Him how much you love Him and make every attempt to put your own needs on the back burner.

There have been times when I have done this and completely laid aside my own burdens, and God still heard my heart and responded to my unmentioned requests. I am convinced that if we approach God like this—He will answer. Does this mean that we should never ask? Of course not! It just means that we have to have a right heart. Before you go to God, get in the habit of asking yourself the question—what is my motive?

Action Plan

Wired to Work Action Plan

Volume 11

Today's Verse/Thought: "Asking for His Will above All Else"

"This is the confidence we have in approaching God: that if we ask anything according to His will, He hears us." *1 John 5:14*

Life Implication:

We have all had experiences in life where we have asked for things that were not good for us and been refused. Perhaps it was a parent or guardian who was looking out for our best interest and knew that what we were asking for was either not possible or not something that would be healthy for us at the time.

Usually when we ask for something we have already made up our minds that it is worthy. Because of the presupposition that is now there, it is difficult to understand why we don't get it. We feel rejected, but we must remember that it is our selfish attitude that may be in the way. We must also remember that God's will is always better than our own.

Life Application: (What I Must *Do*)

When Jesus asked His Father to "take this cup from Me," in Mark 14:36, He was considering the great pain He was about to endure for you and me on that cross. But, on the heels of that request He continued, "not what I will, but what You will." In other words, not withstanding the pain here—the thing that is most important Lord, is Your will.

I wonder if we will be surprised some day to discover how many times we jumped in and just demanded that God answer our requests. Perhaps we wanted Him to heal in a certain situation and nothing happened. Keep in mind that God's idea of broken is very different than ours. We can never presume to know what God may be doing in a given situation. Remember to always begin by asking for His will in a given matter. The next volume will deal with our privilege in prayer to come against the forces that may be at cross-purposes with His will.

Action Plan

Wired to Work Action Plan
Volume 12

Today's Verse/Thought: "Coming against the Forces at Work"

"I have given you authority to trample on snakes and scorpions and to overcome all the power of the enemy . . ." *Luke 10:19*

Life Implication:

There are four forces at work in our life all the time: The *world*, our *flesh*, the *devil,* and the *Lord.* It is the latter force (the Lord) that we want more of. Discerning the other three can at times be difficult. Once we have prayed for God's will to be realized, we must then consider the forces that may be at work in a given situation. Not recognizing and praying against these negative forces can give them a place of power.

The Bible says that we have not because we ask not. This is where we need to understand our responsibility. God is calling us to recognize and come against anything in our life that may be contrary to His will.

Life Application: (What I Must *Do*)

Because of Jesus' shed blood on the cross, you and I have been given the power and the authority to pray against the forces that may be at cross purposes with God's will. What are those forces? The *world* the *flesh* and the *devil.*

You and I can go before God with confidence and pray against these forces. Sometimes it is a matter of living in a fallen world where our environment, with it's numerous diseases, are destroying us. Other times it is our flesh with its self-centered bent on satisfying it's limitless desires. And then there is the devil. We must remember that the devil is real and he hates us. Go before God and pray aggressively against these forces in your situation. If you do this faithfully, you can then walk away from your prayer time with the confidence that you have done your part. Then relax and remember that He knows what is best.

Action Plan

____

____

____

____

____

____

____

____

____

____

____

____

____

____

____

____

____

Wired to Work Action Plan
Volume 13

Today's Verse/Thought: "Unalterable Fact 1—He Knows Me and Has a Purpose"

"Before I formed you in the womb I knew you, before you were born I set you apart; I appointed you as a prophet to the nations." *Jeremiah 1:5*

Life Implication:

Whether you know God or not you have likely sensed some sort of destiny or purpose for your life. We were created that way and God's great desire is that some day we discover His perfect plan for us.

Not knowing His plan for our life leaves us to following the plans outlined by the world around us, or our own inclinations. This can often lead to a sense of frustration. Nothing is as important as knowing and living out our Creator's purpose.

Life Application: (What I Must *Do*)

What God spoke to Jeremiah in the verse above is something that He wants to say to all of us. In Jeremiah's case He was appointing him as a prophet. He has a plan for each one of us too.

If you are having difficulty discovering God's plan for your life—you are not alone. Most people have a difficult time here. As we have already mentioned, getting close to God is the key to everything. Go to Him in prayer everyday and ask Him to specifically reveal His plan for your life. I can't underscore enough the need to be specific. Be persistent and then sit back and watch for His response.

It might be a person He sends with a subtle message or idea. It could be an opportunity or circumstance that He sends your way. Look at everything that comes along—chance meeting—phone appointments—trips to the market, etc. as possible scenarios where God might be communicating something to you.

Action Plan

Wired to Work Action Plan
Volume 14

Today's Verse/Thought: "Unalterable Fact 2—I Have Special Gifts"

"Just as each of us has one body with many members, and these members do not all have the same function, so in Christ we who are many form one body, and each member belongs to all the others. We have different gifts, according to the grace given us . . ." *Romans 12:4-6*

Life Implication:

You are not the accidental evolution of pond scum. God has marvelously and uniquely fashioned you. You are special and have been given gifts by a loving God who is equipping you for a unique task.

Most people never discover their God-given gifts. In Romans we read about the seven natural or personal gifts that are given to all of us. Knowing which of these God has given you is critical to your understanding of how He wants to direct your life.

Life Application: (What I Must *Do*)

Ask God in prayer every day to help you discover your natural gifts. Sometimes our learned behavior or gifts blur our understanding of God's natural gifting in us. Now that you have completed the natural gift test, ask God to confirm the results. Look for opportunities to use your gifts. Sometimes in the exercising of your gifts God reveals His greater purpose.

Ask others what they think your gifts are and note their responses. Start with your family. Then go to those you work with, friends, neighbors and people in your church. Often others see us in ways we cannot.

Action Plan

Wired to Work Action Plan
Volume 15

Today's Verse/Thought: "Unalterable Fact 3—He Wants Me to Know"

"I pray also that the eyes of your heart may be enlightened in order that you may know the hope to which He has called you, the riches of His glorious inheritance in the saints . . ." *Ephesians 1:18*

Life Implication:

God's greatest desire is for you and I to truly know Him, and then as a result, discover the wonderful plan He has for our life. I don't know about you, but I do not want to be among those who never "get it," who never discover God's unique plan for their life.

Not living out His plan for your life is called existence. Existence can be okay—even fun, but when we do not choose God's best I believe we miss something special. There is a tremendous sense of frustration associated with living life on a level less than His highest.

Life Application: (What I Must *Do*)

Every morning ask God to open a new opportunity or experience that will help you to live your life according to His plan. Ask Him to enlighten your heart and to help you see yourself through His eyes. Lord, when You look at me what do You see?

As we learned in volume 14, discovering your own specific gifts is critical to this process. After discovering your natural gifts, begin to ask God to develop and use those gifts within the settings He has placed you. Ask Him to take His vision for your life and begin to work it into your DNA.

Action Plan

Wired to Work Action Plan

Volume 16

Today's Verse/Thought: "Now That I Know—What Should I Do?"

"It's like a man going away: He leaves his house and puts his servants in charge, each with his assigned task, and tells the one at the door to keep watch. 'Therefore keep watch because you do not know when the owner of the house will come back—whether in the evening, or at midnight, or when the rooster crows, or at dawn. If he comes suddenly, do not let him find you sleeping. What I say to you, I say to everyone: 'Watch!' " *Mark 13:34-36*

Life Implication:

The above verses make it clear that we are to *work* (our assigned task) and *watch*. In the process of discovering our purpose, we must also prepare ourselves. We must be alert to the world around us.

Most Christians today know very little about what is going on outside of their small circle. This can be very dangerous. As Christians we should make every effort to prepare ourselves physically, mentally and spiritually for the rest of our journey.

Life Application: (What I Must *Do*)

As you continue to find God's purpose for your life, make yourself a student of the environment around you. Keep abreast of current affairs and know how the world around you thinks. Pick up reading material that will help you in this area.

You may want to use the web or your local Christian bookstore (authors like George Barna, Chuck Colson) to uncover additional sources of information. Position yourself to begin the all-important process of *watching*. Remember, a successful soldier knows every aspect of the battlefield.

Action Plan

Wired to Work Action Plan
Volume 17

Today's Verse/Thought: "Finding the Way—Vision"

"If you do not know where you are going—any road will take you there."

Life Implication:

The Bible says in Proverbs, "Where there is no *vision* . . . the people perish." I like the NIV version that states, "Where there is no *revelation* . . . the people cast off restraint." In other words, if you do not know where you are going . . . any road will take you there.

I believe that most failure, whether business, marital or personal, can be traced back to a lack of vision. A lack of vision may just be the single biggest contributor to suicide. Every human being desperately needs a reason for being. This is what separates us from any other creature on earth.

Life Application: (What I Must *Do*)

Take stock of your life. Make a list of all your significant experiences. Think about your interests and write them down. Now, consider your passion—what moves you emotionally? Sometimes by reviewing these areas God begins to reveal a pattern. At the very least, go before Him with this information and ask Him what it all means.

The Lord will oftentimes allow us to experience significant events in life for a specific reason. Be patient. Hab. 2:3 says "For the revelation awaits an appointed time; it speaks of the end and will not prove false. Though it linger, wait for it; it will certainly come and will not delay."

Finally, be sure to line up the "four factors" outlined in the following volumes before you step out. These factors will clearly indicate whether you are following God's *vision* or your own.

Action Plan

___

___

___

___

___

___

___

___

___

___

___

___

___

___

___

___

___

___

Wired to Work Action Plan
Volume 18

Today's Verse/Thought: "Lining Up the Factors 1—Is It in the Word?"

"Your word is a lamp to my feet and a light for my path." *Psalm 119:105*

Life Implication:

There are four factors that need to line up before you can be sure that it is God who is calling you into a particular direction: 1) Are you reading it in the His Word? 2) Are you hearing it by His Spirit? 3) Is it being affirmed through wise, godly counsel? 4) And, is it consistent with current circumstances?

When God calls us to a certain direction or vision He will always reveal it to us through His Word. An excellent guideline is to remain still until a clear pattern becomes evident during your regular times of reading the bible.

Remember that Psalm 119:105 contains two promises. Not only will His Word be a lamp to your feet—illuminating your daily steps, but it will also become a light to your path—a bright light focused on the place where He is taking you. You will never see God's vision for your life unless you are reading His Word.

Life Application: (What I Must *Do*)

Pray and read your bible every day. Ask God to reveal His plan to you through the written Word. Have a pen and paper handy and take note of anything you think may be jumping off the pages at you.

After some time go back over your notes or the places you may have underlined in your bible and see if there is a pattern there. I find this to be very helpful. If you notice a pattern, remember that this is just one of the four factors. Don't step out yet—read on . . .

Action Plan

____

____

____

____

____

____

____

____

____

____

____

____

____

____

____

____

____

____

____

____

____

Wired to Work Action Plan
Volume 19

Today's Verse/Thought: "Lining Up the Factors 2—What Am I Hearing?"

"Whether you turn to the right or to the left, your ears will hear a voice behind you, saying, 'This is the way; walk in it.' " *Isaiah 30:21*

Life Implication:

Hearing God is essential to our moving on, yet it is one of the most difficult things to do. Our minds are so active that it is almost impossible to get quiet and sensitive enough to hear His voice.

If you are not hearing God—then don't move forward—wait. I am not talking about an audible voice. God will usually whisper something to your heart and you will know it is Him because it will be something that your mind probably never would have thought of. At least that's how it works for me.

Life Application: (What I Must *Do*)

Be still. Praise Him. Pray and ask Him to speak to you. Wait patiently to hear His voice. Pray and promise Him that you will not move forward until you do. Keep your paper and pen handy and jot down thoughts or ideas you feel might be coming from Him. Compare what you are hearing to what you are reading. See if there is a pattern.

As I mentioned before, though you may see a pattern, remember that this may be just one or two of the four factors. It's not time to take action yet—read on . . .

Action Plan

Wired to Work Action Plan
Volume 20

Today's Verse/Thought: "Lining Up the Factors 3—Affirming with Counsel"

"Plans fail for lack of counsel, but with many advisers they succeed." *Proverbs 15:22*

Life Implication:

There is nothing worse then going through life bent on having it your way. We need each other for advice and counsel. This is true in business, family situations, church and especially with regard to finding God's plan for your life.

Unless what God is saying to you is being affirmed through wise, godly counsel—don't move ahead!

Life Application: (What I Must *Do*)

Consider all of what God may be revealing to you through the Word, His voice and your circumstances and submit them to godly people who will pray and give you their advice. God is not a God of disorder. If it is Him, then He will affirm it through others.

The key is to find mature believers who will pray and seek God on your behalf. Your job is to pray that they receive clear and divine counsel. Depending upon the magnitude of your decision I suggest involving at least three or four trustworthy believers or couples. Be sure not to include anyone who may be impacted by the outcome.

Action Plan

____

____

____

Wired to Work Action Plan
Volume 21

Today's Verse/Thought: "Lining Up the Factors 4—What about Circumstances?"

"In Him we were also chosen, having been predestined according to the plan of Him who works out everything in conformity with the purpose of His will." *Ephesians 1:11*

Life Implication:

Ignoring our circumstances and venturing out in a new direction can often devastate our life and the lives of those around us. While it is true that God allows things to happen in our life—both good and bad—He is not necessarily the cause. God can redeem any situation—even the ones we stumble our way into.

It is very important that we carefully consider our circumstances before taking any kind of significant step. The fact that you may have just lost your job may not be a clear sign that God wants you to move to Africa and be a missionary. It may just be that you lost your job. This is why all four factors should be considered and not just one or two.

Life Application: (What I Must *Do*)

If you are noticing a pattern in the Word, if you are hearing His voice and your chosen counsel is affirming, then examine your circumstances. Ask yourself, where does God have me right now? How will your decisions affect others? Do you have the resources necessary to move out in the way you believe He is calling you?

Remember that when it comes to resources there is a fine line between faith and foolishness. Let me remind you again that God is a God of order. If He is calling you—then all four factors will line up. I have witnessed this in my own life and have yet to see it fail in others.

Action Plan

Wired to Work Action Plan
Volume 22

Today's Verse/Thought: "Being Like Christ 1—BehaviorThat Lights Up"

"You are the light of the world. A city on a hill cannot be hidden. Neither do people light a lamp and put it under a bowl. Instead they put it on its stand, and it gives light to everyone in the house. In the same way, *let* your light shine before men, that they may see your good deeds and praise your Father in heaven." *Matthew 5:14-16*

Life Implication:

The Bible makes it clear that we are called to be lights. It does not tell us to shine our light on people—but to allow our light to shine. When we shine our light others only see the glare. This is a clear call to "walk the walk" and not just "talk the talk."

Remember the great painting of the Mona Lisa. I doubt you could describe what that frame looks like. The job of a good frame is not to draw attention to itself, but rather the precious content it is meant to display.

Are people seeing Jesus *in* you—or are they seeing you—the frame? Unless Jesus' nature is revealed in us we will have little foundation to speak with authority about Him. The big problem today with many Christians is that we just want to talk about Jesus. That is why our *real* witness is so weak. I call it "sound-bite" Christianity.

We cannot compromise. If we are followers of Christ then we must live exemplary lives. That means that we do not have the liberty to cheat or stretch the truth in any area. Anything less will virtually disqualify us from being worthy of witnessing for Him. The world is looking for the *real* deal. We must give it to them.

Life Application: (What I Must *Do*)

Examine your life. Are there areas where you are compromising? Make a list of what you will have to let go of in order to be all that Jesus wants. Pray and give those issues in your life to God. Make a commitment to rid yourself of all that hinders you.

Are you shining your light or letting it shine? Are you IMposing or EXposing your faith? Are you planting seeds or pulling weeds? Telling people about Jesus is only effective if we have earned our place on the platform.

Action Plan

Wired to Work Action Plan
Volume 23

Today's Verse/Thought: "Being Like Christ 2—Attitude Adjustment"

"But I tell you who hear me: Love your enemies, do good to those who hate you, bless those who curse you, pray for those who mistreat you." *Luke 6:27-28*

Life Implication:

Jesus would not have told us to love our enemies if we were never going to have any. We all have enemies—sometimes we know them and sometimes we don't. Enemies are those we do not like or agree with. Jesus says to love them.

One of the biggest reasons why Christians do not look any different from the rest of the world is because we fail to live up to this command. Jesus loved and was able to see the potential in everyone. He expects the same from us. The Bible tells us not to judge others. Having a wrong attitude toward those we do not like or agree with can have a detrimental affect on our own spiritual well being.

Life Application: (What I Must *Do*)

Do you find yourself telling off color jokes about others? Maybe they are political leaders or people you struggle with in life. As a believer in Jesus we cannot allow ourself this liberty. Decide to rid yourself of all such slander.

Make a list of the people who may be your enemies. Next to each name list an action item—something you know you need to do. It might be asking someone to lunch and having a heart-to-heart talk with them. Perhaps you need to ask someone to forgive you for the way you have been thinking or the things you have said.

Begin to pray for each of these people on your list. Ask God to show you how He would have you pray.

Proverbs 16:3 says that if we commit our *works* (behavior) to the Lord—then our *thoughts* (attitude) will be established. Having a healthy attitude about people is critical and requires us to be proactive.

Action Plan

Wired to Work Action Plan
Volume 24

Today's Verse/Thought: "Being Like Christ 3—Leaving the Comfort Zone"

"The Reubenites and Gadites, who had very large herds and flocks, saw that the lands of Jazer and Gilead were suitable for livestock. So they came to Moses and Eleazar the priest and to the leaders of the community, and said, 'Ataroth, Dibon, Jazer, Nimrah, Heshbon, Elealeh, Sebam, Nebo, and Beon. The land the LORD subdued before the people of Israel are suitable for livestock, and your servants have livestock. If we have found favor in your eyes,' they said, 'let this land be given to your servants as our possession. Do not make us cross the Jordan.' Moses said to the Gadites and Reubenites, 'Shall your countrymen go to war while you sit here? Why do you discourage the Israelites from going over into the land the LORD has given them?' " *Numbers 32:1-7*

Life Implication:

It is so tempting to get comfortable where we are and not want to step out. Especially when the consequences are uncertain. If we do not step out of our comfort zone two things will never occur: 1) Some of what God may want us to accomplish will not get done, and 2) We will not be stretched. God uses the challenges in life to grow us. If we sit still—we will not grow.

Life Application: (What I Must *Do*)

Determine not to let any lack of confidence in your own ability keep you from stepping out. Just like the example of Jesus feeding the five thousand using just a little boy with a few loaves and fish—He wants to do the same through us. That little boy knew he did not have enough. Neither do we. The miracle happens when we step out anyway. Jesus says I am looking for your obedience—not your ability. Remember—He is able.

Are there areas where you have been afraid to step out of your comfort zone? Take them to God in prayer and ask Him to show you what to do. Avoid the trap of thinking—who am I? What can one person do? Remember that if you want to grow you will have to be stretched. Making mistakes is part of the process.

Oswald Chambers says, "Never let the sense of past failure corrupt your new action."

Action Plan

____

____

____

____

____

____

____

____

____

____

____

____

____

____

Wired to Work Action Plan
Volume 25

Today's Verse/Thought: "Being Like Christ 4—The End in View"

"With malice toward none; with charity for all; with firmness in the right, as God gives us to see the right—let us strive on to finish the work we are in." *Abraham Lincoln (1809–65), U.S. president. Second Inaugural Address, 4 March 1865.*

Life Implication:

In the game of golf I have noticed the meticulous attention that a golfer will give to every aspect of the course. They carefully take into consideration the lay of the land, the curves and firmness of the ground and the precise distance to the hole. This enables them to select just the right club for that all-important shot.

We need to understand the implications this model holds for us. A golfer always keeps the end in view. They know that sometimes you have to chip out from behind an obstacle and lose a stroke in order to achieve the greater gain. In life it is important for us to do the same. We need to keep the end in sight. What is the greater purpose?

Life Application: (What I Must *Do*)

If you calculate your life-course like a golfer calculates the green, you will find yourself making better decisions. Sometimes in relating to your spouse or child you need a putter—and you've got the driver out. And sometimes you will have to give some ground in order to realize the higher purpose.

Take a look at what lies in front of you. Be aware of the obstacles, but don't let them overwhelm you. Remember that God wants you to see a greater purpose.

Think about handling your challenge in light of how it will help you advance. Hold onto the *vision*. Ask God every day to show you which club to use. He will!

Action Plan

Wired to Work Action Plan
Volume 26

Today's Verse/Thought: "Accountable Relationships"

"Brothers, if someone is caught in a sin, you who are spiritual should restore him gently. But watch yourself, or you also may be tempted. Carry each other's burdens, and in this way you will fulfill the law of Christ." *Galatians 6:1-3*

Life Implication:

We all have burdens and tough stuff that we deal with in life. If we try to go-it-alone, oftentimes we succumb to the pressures of the world the flesh and the devil. We need each other. The above verse admonishes us to *carry each other's burdens.* I cannot carry your burden if I do not know what it is.

The devil does a good job with some of us—convincing us that we are the only ones who think or behave that way. It is a lie that is not easy to cast aside unless we are actively helping each other.

Life Application: (What I Must *Do*)

Find one or more persons right now with whom you can be accountable. Be careful not to mix gender, keep it—men with men—women with women. If you are not already in a small group or discipling relationship then ask God to bring someone to you to begin the process. After sharing your areas of need and struggle give them permission to ask you some difficult questions.

No matter how mature you are in your relationship with God—you will always need this kind of accountability in your life. The moment you think you have arrived—you no longer have need for accountability. Destruction lies ahead . . . you can count on it!

"And let us consider how we may spur one another on toward love and good deeds." *Hebrews 10:24*

Action Plan

Wired to Work Action Plan

Volume 27

Today's Verse/Thought: "Consistency—the Goal"

"Let your eyes look straight ahead, fix your gaze directly before you. Make level paths for your feet and take only ways that are firm." *Proverbs 4:25-26*

Life Implication:

I love this verse. It is so powerful—*fix your gaze*—the idea of vision. *Take only ways that are firm*—the concept of stability. I am especially drawn to the words, *make level paths for your feet.* Here we have the powerful picture of being on a *level* path. To me this represents consistency—or—avoiding life's ups and downs.

The roller coaster of life will drag you down and wear you out. Many Christians want to live on a spiritual mountaintop all the time, but the inevitable valley of negative circumstances has a way of bringing us down. We need to discover ways to flatten out our journey in order to stay fresh for the long haul.

Life Application: (What I Must *Do*)

Are you just looking for the mountain peak experiences? Or are you having a difficult time escaping the valley? Ask God to help you find that level path for your life. This is a great area to engage your accountability partners. I find that when I am open and transparent with others, they can often help me find that more consistent walk.

No one can live on the top of the mountain. The excitement and lack of oxygen will eventually destroy you. God loves to bring us there occasionally for our edification and perspective. You can see a lot from up there. Our reality, however, is on the plains. That is where God wants us to live. Get used to it. Pursue it. See it as a positive thing and look for God to do mighty things through you, regardless of where you are.

Action Plan

Wired to Work Action Plan
Volume 28

Today's Verse/Thought: "I Love You ____________"

"For God so loved the world that he gave his one and only Son, that whoever believes in Him shall not perish but have eternal life." *John 3:16*

Life Implication:

John 3:16 is the most quoted verse in the whole Bible. God loved us so much that He sacrificed His own Son. The biggest tragedy I can think of is to go through life never understanding how much God loves us.

Sometimes if we have difficulty understanding our heavenly Father's love we put unnecessary pressure on earthly relationships. Today, many people suffer from what has been called a "father vacuum." This is a condition that occurs as the result of either no relationship with our earthly dad—or a dysfunctional one. Unless you understand and appropriate God's love you will never be able to overcome such tragic conditions.

I Love You ____________

Life Application: (What I Must *Do*)

Write your name in the space above and complete the most powerful four words in all of life. Now look at it—look again. Believe it—God is telling you how much He loves you. No matter where you've been—what you've done—you are precious to Him.

Keep in mind that He does not care what anyone else may think about you—He doesn't even care what you think about you. He loves you with a love that goes so far beyond anything you can comprehend. Write those four words down and keep them with your daily devotional materials. Read them often and then tell Him how much they mean to you.

Action Plan

Wired to Work Action Plan

Volume 29

Today's Verse/Thought: "My Plans Are Good"

" 'For I know the plans I have for you,' declares the LORD, 'plans to prosper you and not to harm you, plans to give you hope and a future.' " *Jeremiah 29:11*

Life Implication:

This entire book has been about understanding *how* and *why* God made us. He made us for a purpose—He has a plan for your life. God says that His plan is to prosper you and not to harm you.

As amazing as this promise is, it will never be realized if you fail to apply it to your life. You cannot enter into God's plan if you are wallowing around in the "what-might-have-beens" of life.

Life Application: (What I Must *Do*)

If you are stuck on past failures say to yourself what I am sure the Apostle Paul would say if he were here—GET OVER IT! Were there any number of course corrections in your life because you blew it along the way? You bet. Does that hinder God in any way from starting a new course—right now? No!

God is not limited by our past mistakes. Believe it or not—it's your choice. The Father sent His son Jesus to die on a cross for you and me to once and for all draw a line in the sand that separates us from our past. He has said, MY PLANS ARE GOOD! Four powerful words . . . that begin right now!

Action Plan

____

____

____

____

____

____

____

____

____

____

____

____

____

____

____

____

____

____

____

____

____

Wired to Work Action Plan
Volume 30

Today's Verse/Thought: "Stay Close to Me"

"Come near to God and He will come near to you." *James 4:8*

Life Implication:

I have repeated the above verse several times throughout this book. It is the secret to understanding how an invisible God can love us like He does—the key to discovering His plan for our life—summed up in four powerful words . . . STAY CLOSE TO ME.

God would say to us today that the weapons of warfare and the armor of protection that will be required of us in the battle yet to come are so totally unconventional that we can't even conceive of them with today's mind. The key is to stay close to Him.

Life Application: (What I Must *Do*)

Eleven powerful words draw us to the conclusion:

I LOVE YOU
MY PLANS ARE GOOD
STAY CLOSE TO ME

If you remember nothing else about this exercise please commit these words to memory. I have them written down in several prominent locations as a constant reminder. My friend, the battle is heating up. God wants to use you. If you do not want to be a casualty, but rather a victorious warrior for God—heed His words and hold to these promises.

Action Plan

Personal Notes